Christification

Christification

A Lutheran Approach to Theosis

Jordan Cooper

WIPF & STOCK · Eugene, Oregon

CHRISTIFICATION
A Lutheran Approach to Theosis

Wipf and Stock
An Imprint of Wipf and Stock Publishers
199 W. 8th Ave., Suite 3
EUGENE, OR 97401

www.wipfandstock.com

ISBN 13: 978-1-62564-616-3

Manufactured in the U.S.A.   07/03/2014

A version of some of the content contained herein has been published as: Cooper, Jordan. Just and Sinner (blog) http://www.justandsinner.com. Used by permission.

To Herb Greenspan, who first urged me to
study deification in the Eastern tradition.

Contents

Abbreviations

AC	The Augsburg Confession
ANF	*Ante-Nicene Fathers*
Apol	Apology of the Augsburg Confession
FC Ep	The Epitome of the Formula of Concord
FC SD	The Solid Declaration of the Formula of Concord
LC	The Large Catechism
LW	*Luther's Works*
NPNF[1]	*Nicene and Post-Nicene Fathers*, Series 1
NPNF[2]	*Nicene and Post-Nicene Fathers*, Series 2
SA	The Smalcald Articles
SC	The Small Catechism
WA	Weimarer Ausgabe

All references to the Lutheran Confessions are taken from Kolb, Robert, and Timothy J. Wengert, eds. *The Book of Concord: The Confessions of the Evangelical Lutheran Church.* Translated by Charles Arand, et al. Minneapolis: Fortress, 2000.

Introduction

THEOSIS, OR "DEIFICATION," is a prominent teaching in the history of the church. Though predominantly associated with the East, notions of participation in divinity are apparent in the great Western traditions as well. Such language is present in the literature from Ignatius of Antioch to John the Damascene and from Martin Luther to Robert Jenson. Recent years have seen a resurgence of the doctrine of deification. The early to mid-twentieth century saw a revival of the thought of Gregory Palamas within Eastern Orthodoxy by the Neopalamite theological school led by Vladimir Lossky. This involved a recapturing of a distinctively Eastern theology, which emphasized deification and mystical theology over the Scholastic tendencies of the West. In the 1970s, a school of Finnish Luther scholars following Tuomo Mannermaa discovered something of a doctrine of theosis in the writings of Luther, especially in his 1535 Galatians commentary. This discovery has allowed Lutherans to have more productive conversations with the Eastern Church; many purport that the soteriologies of Luther and the East are compatible with one another. There have also been recent attempts to argue for theosis within the theology of John Calvin and John Wesley, leading to a discovery of the doctrine within Baptist, Presbyterian, Anglican, and Methodist traditions.

This has, I think, been a positive movement within the church. With all of the divergences over the doctrine of justification since the Reformation, there is need for a soteriological starting point that can promote productive ecumenical dialogue, and deification is a doctrine that is truly catholic. That being said, the various theological traditions are not willing to simply admit agreement here by dismissing all their various other disagreements with a feigned unity of faith, nor should they. Indeed, there are many differences of opinion even on the doctrine of theosis itself. In the East, deification is the primary soteriological motif, eclipsing any discussion of forensic justification. In the Lutheran tradition, theosis can, at most, be viewed as a compatible and secondary soteriological category; justification is the "doctrine upon which the church stands or falls."[1]

I propose that a thoroughly Reformational understanding of justification can coexist with a patristic understanding of theosis. For too long, theologians and exegetes have pitted legal and ontological soteric categories against one another, casting salvation as either about imputation or ontological renewal. This false dichotomy has built up walls between theological traditions that need not exist. A consistently and uncompromisingly biblical theology necessitates that salvation includes forensic justification along with a real-ontic union with God and participation in Trinitarian life.

---

1. *Quia isto articulo stante stat Ecclesia, ruente ruit Ecclesia* (WA 40.III.352).

1

Defining Theosis

THEOSIS IS A MULTIFACETED doctrine with a variety of formulations; thus, it is a difficult concept to define. Most well known is the Athanasian proclamation that "God became man so that man might become god."[1] This statement summarizes the patristic teaching on the subject and establishes a basis on which all further dialogue on the topic expounds. This statement, however, is subject to a variety of interpretations. It could be misread to support the pagan notion of apotheosis, wherein one becomes a unique divine entity among a pantheon of gods. A more precise definition will aid in proceeding with the present work. Though no definition completely captures all the implications and subtleties of this teaching, Norman Russel's explanation of deification is perhaps the most comprehensive:

> Theosis is our restoration as persons to integrity and wholeness by participation in Christ through the Holy Spirit, in a process which is initiated in this world through our life of ecclesial communion and moral striving and finds ultimate fulfillment in our union with the Father— all within the broad context of the divine economy.[2]

While the Lutheran tradition has placed soteriology primarily in the realm of event rather than process, the Eastern tradition proclaims deification, its central soteriological category, as a process.

---

1. Athanasius, *On the Incarnation*, 54.
2. Russell, *Fellow Workers with God*, 21.

1

Salvation as Process in Orthodox and Lutheran Theology

Notions of salvation as event and process need not be pitted against one another. Justification, in Lutheran (and Pauline) theology, is an event of the past and present, in which God's eschatological verdict of "righteous" is placed on his people in advance. This occurs through the alien righteousness of Christ received by faith.[3] As will be demonstrated below, the Lutheran Confessions are also willing to speak of a soteric process by which union with God is increased and the believer progresses in holiness. This is the context in which theosis is to be placed.

Such a distinction between event and process is not foreign to Orthodox theology either. In his popular handbook on the Orthodox Church, Anthony Coniaris distinguishes between justification and sanctification. He defines justification as the understanding that "we have been saved from sin and death through baptism, which is our personal Golgotha."[4] In Coniaris' perspective, justification is the beginning of the Christian life—salvation spoken of in the past tense. Justification is received by faith, which is "the humble acceptance of God's gracious gift. It is the hand that takes the blessing. It receives what God gives, not as something we deserve, but as a gift of His grace."[5] Good works do not cause justification, but are "a grateful response, a feeble attempt on our part to show appreciation to God for what He has done for us."[6] This is distinguished from sanctification, which is the understanding that "we are being saved daily as we repent of our sins and continue to walk with Jesus yielding our will to Him in humble obedience."[7] Like Luther, Coniaris speaks of conversion and repentance as a daily reality. The great saints "were not converted once. Nor did they repent just once. Their life was a daily conversion and a constant

3. See Cooper, "Lutheran Response to Justification."
4. Coniaris, *Introducing Orthodox Church*, 55.
5. Ibid.
6. Ibid., 52–53.
7. Ibid., 55.

repentance."[8] If Coniaris is representative of Orthodox theology in this regard, there are many convergences between Lutheran and Orthodox soteriology. For both, salvation can be spoken of in the past tense in relation to justification. This occurs through faith and baptism, wherein God creates life from death and gives the forgiveness of sins due to the work of Christ at Golgotha. Works then serve as the result of God's grace, in thankfulness for what God has done in Christ. Theosis is then placed alongside of justification as a compatible soteriological motif. It flows from justification and involves a process of growth.

The difference, then, between the two traditions is not over whether salvation is an event or a process, but over which aspect of redemption is primary. Orthodox theology, especially since Lossky's critique of Western theology, has emphasized salvation as a process.[9] The doctrine of justification has received little to no treatment in major orthodox dogmatic works. Lutheran theology emphasizes salvation as an event—as justification. Though some may claim this to be merely the outgrowth of medieval debates or as an overreaction to Semipelagianism, there are important theological reasons for this prioritization. In justification, one receives the benefits of Christ: namely, the forgiveness of sins and the righteousness of Christ. God's eschatological verdict is placed upon the sinner in the present, resulting in the justification of the ungodly. This work is perfect in the present life, and assures the eternal salvation of God's people. Growth is always incomplete; the Christian will always remain *simul iustus et peccator* because he or she simultaneously exists in eschatological life and the present Adamic age. The Christian is a citizen of both this age and the age to come. One progresses toward union with God as eschatological life moves toward the believer, and the old Adam is put to death. If the focus were on salvation as a process—in terms of sanctification or deification—one's assurance would be misplaced. It is always the perfect act of God, rather than the imperfect and continual,

8. Ibid., 48.

9. See Lossky's critique of Anselm's legal approach to redemption in Lossky, *Likeness of God*, 99–103.

which gives the assurance of salvation and which then serves as the basis for theosis.

Becoming God

The notion of "becoming god" falls deaf on Western ears. It likely brings up images of ancient hero cults in which a great figure, emperor, or pharaoh was said to become a divine figure. Or perhaps the Mormon conception of divinization comes to mind, under which a man can genuinely become a god, not merely through participation but in essence. Such misconceptions need to be clarified before proceeding. A distinction, which the fathers were careful to make, must be drawn between theosis and apotheosis.[10] Apotheosis is the notion that a human can become a divine entity—that a complete ontological transformation takes place wherein humanity is transcended and becomes god by nature. This would displace the Trinitarian God and result in pantheism. Andrew Louth writes that:

> Here is perhaps a good place to clear up a misconception about deification, namely, that it involves the transformation of our human nature into something other than human, some kind of apotheosis that removes our humanity: to quote some frequently quoted words, "If the aim of the Christian is to cease to be 'human, all too human,' it would be a natural corollary in Christology to regard the humanity of our Lord as a problem rather than a datum." For the Orthodox tradition, and for St. Maximus in particular, nothing could be further from the truth: the aim of the Christian is to become once again truly human, to become the human partners of God as we

10. "The mystical union between God and humans is a true union, yet in this union Creator and creature do not become fused into a single being. Unlike the eastern religions, which teach that humans are swallowed up in the deity, Orthodox *Mystical Theology* has always insisted that we humans, however closely linked to God, retain our full personal integrity. The human person, when deified, remains distinct (though not separate) from God" (Ware, *Orthodox Church*, 232).

were originally created, and as human partners to share
in the divine life.[11]

Deification thus involves the restoration of mankind's original creation. Adam was created to share in God's own life, but forfeited that life through sin. Through theosis, humanity once again
regains that participation; there is no dissolution of human nature,
but a more complete human nature.

There is a distinction at work in this concept between nature and grace. Humanity does not become in any sense divinized
by nature; that would imply an identity with the divine essence
and would violate the creature/Creator distinction inherent in
orthodox Christian theology. It is only by grace that humankind
can participate in divinity and share in God's Trinitarian life. This
secures the qualitative distinction between Creator and creature.
God is the giver of grace, life, and salvation; humanity is simply the
recipient. As Keating writes, "Properly understood, the Christian
doctrine of deification not only maintains the distinction between
God and the created order, but is premised on it. Christian deification dissolves if the fundamental difference between what is divine
and what is human is compromised."[12] To have a person, thing, or
essence, and to state that one can participate in that person, thing,
or essence, necessarily implies that there is a fundamental differentiation between the identity of the one who participates and
the thing that is participated in. This is the case in the Orthodox
doctrine of deification.[13]

---

11. Louth, *Theosis in Orthodox Theology*, 39.

12. Keating, *Deification and Grace*, 92.

13. Keating writes, "More significantly, if God is the source of all being,
then we as creatures participate in his being. We do not share or participate
in the divine being as God himself possesses it. Rather, we share in his being
in that he gives us our created being by bringing us into existence. He has it
essentially; we have it derivatively and by participation. He is being; we participate in being. Participation is a way of speaking about how 'in him we live and
move and have our being' (Acts 17:28)" (ibid., 97).

Image and Likeness

Many Orthodox theologians utilize a distinction from Irenaeus between humanity's creation in the image of God, and the likeness of God.[14] Adam was created with both the likeness and image of God. Through the fall, the likeness was lost, but the image retained. The likeness is regained through grace, as a central soteriological reality. This distinction emphasizes both the reality of the fall and preserves the goodness of mankind as creation. In other words, humanity, though fallen, is not beyond redemption.

Lossky has written extensively on this topic, and his approach has significantly influenced contemporary Orthodox dialogue on the subject. Lossky argues that the image of God is a holistic motif that encapsulates the entirety of mankind, body and soul. In fact, rather than privileging the soul over the body, Palamas is willing to argue that humanity is "more in the image of God"[15] than angels are, precisely because of because we inhabit bodies. Although Lossky does not dismiss patristic attempts to identify the image with various aspects of human mind, body, and soul, he argues that essentially the image of God in man is unknowable.[16] This conviction flows from Lossky's apophaticism, taken from Pseudo-Dionysius. Apophatic theology purports that God's essence is unknowable. God is known by way of negation rather than positive affirmation because God's being is beyond what can be captured by any locutionary act. Similarly, God's image in humankind must also be, in essence, unknowable. Lossky writes, "The image of God in man, insofar as it is perfect, is necessarily unknowable, according to St. Gregory of Nyssa; for as it reflects the fullness of the archetype, it must also possess the unknowable character of the

---

14. "The word 'likeness' as used in the Septuagint, expresses something dynamic and not yet realized, whereas the word 'image' signifies a realized state, which the present context constitutes the starting point for the attainment of 'likeness,'" (Mantzaridēs, *Deification of Man*, 21).

15. Lossky, *Mystical Theology*, 116.

16. Ibid., 118.

divine Being."[17] This view is supported by the fact that Scripture, while speaking often about the *imago Dei*, never defines it.[18]

Lossky argues that the image is not lost by the fall, but is greatly diminished. He claims that "God's image in man attains its perfection only when human nature becomes like God's nature, when it begins fully to participate in uncreated goodness."[19] The image is retained through the exercise of free will.[20] The human agent has the ability to move toward God, resulting in the renewal of the image through deification, or move away from God, resulting in a diminished image. The Eastern Church does not view the prelapsarian state in the same manner as the West. There is no state of "original righteousness," but Adam and Eve were created with potential. Adam was created with a specific mission, which was to unite all of creation and assist in its deification. The divisions that exist as an aspect of creation are not meant to be permanent, for Adam was to fulfill his vocation by uniting division in participation with divine life.[21] This would occur through a process wherein Adam was to be deified, and through him, all of creation would experience theosis. There is a conviction inherent in this model that grace is a necessary addition to creation *ex nihilo*. Creation, therefore, does not share the quality of goodness as such, but only through participation in God.[22] The fall is thus not a loss of righteousness, but a change of direction. Instead of a movement

17. Ibid.

18. However, at one point Lossky does write that "in the context of the sacerdotal narrative of Genesis, the creation of man 'in the image' of God confers on human beings a dominion over the animals analogous to that which God enjoys over the whole of his creation" (ibid., *Likeness of God*, 128).

19. Ibid., *Orthodox Theology*, 125.

20. "God becomes powerless before human freedom; He cannot violate it since it flows from His own omnipotence. Certainly man was created by the will of God alone; but he cannot be deified by it alone" (ibid., 73).

21. "Adam must overcome these divisions by a conscious action to reunite in himself the whole of the created cosmos and to become deified with it" (ibid., 74).

22. "The Eastern tradition knows nothing of 'pure nature' to which grace is added as a supernatural gift. For it, there is no natural or 'normal' state, since grace is implied in the act of creation itself" (ibid., *Mystical Theology*, 101).

toward deification, wherein the human creature seeks to unite all things to God, humanity begins focusing on lesser goods, seeking physical rather than spiritual fulfillment.[23]

The goal of redemption, in this anthropological model, is for the likeness of God to be regained in the human creature, and thus the strengthening and renewal of the *imago dei*. This occurs through increasing union with God. Lossky argues that "the image reaches its perfection when the human nature becomes like the divine, in attaining a complete participation in God's uncreated bounty."[24] To be renewed in God's image, human nature must be redeemed through participation in the Trinitarian life and ascend from physical sensory life to spiritual life. Nellas writes, "In fact man, having been created 'in the image' of the infinite God, is called by his own nature—and this is precisely in the sense of 'in the image' from this point of view—to transcend the limited boundaries of creation and to become infinite."[25] In the Eastern view, the definition of humankind is not based on a static essence. One could not, for example, utilize the Aristotelian definition of man as a "rational animal." What defines humanity is not its present state, but its eschatological goal.[26] Deification is thus of the essence of humanity, not merely a response to the fall. Human nature was bound for deification prior to the fall, and redemption brings creation back to that original goal so that all might participate in the divine nature.

23. "Instead of following its natural disposition towards God, the human spirit has turned towards the world; instead of spiritualizing the body it has entered into the stream of animal and sensory life, and become subject to material conditions" (ibid., 131).

24. Ibid., 121.

25. Nellas, *Deification in Christ*, 28.

26. "It thus becomes clear that the essence of man is not found in the matter from which he was created but in the archetype on the basis of which he was formed and towards which he tends" (ibid., 33).

Essence and Energies

Though the earliest formulations of theosis do not make a sharp distinction between God's essence and energies, this manner of speaking has been prominent since the Hesychast controversy of the fourteenth century.[27] The controversy revolved around the nature of one's participation in divinity. For Palamas and the Hesychast school, there is an aspect of God which is transcendent and beyond participation[28] and that is identified with God's essence. To participate in the essence of God is to be God himself. Thus to protect the Creator/creature distinction, Palamas proposed that believers participate not in God's essence, but in his energies. The opposing school, led by Barlaam of Seminara, argued that the proposal of divine energies contradicted Pseudo-Dionysius' apophatic theology. For Barlaam, God is essentially unknowable.

Palamism argues that participation in God's essence is impossible because to participate in an essence is to become the thing itself. If a human creature could somehow participate in God's essence, he or she would by definition *become* God. This would destroy the doctrine of the Trinity, for God would then have as many hypostases as Christians in the world.[29] God's essence is thus both unknowable and imparticipable, both prior to and after the incarnation. These energies were originally identified as the "uncreated light" encountered through theophanic experiences, but were later described as any of the actions of God. For example, all of the anthropomorphisms in Scripture refer not to God in his essence, but to how he acts according to and through his energies. These Eastern theologians reject the Western concept that divine ideas exist within the mind of God according to his essence.[30] These divine ideas, or the divine will, are separate from God's

27. See Ware, *Orthodox Church*, 61–70.

28. See Palamas, *Triads*.

29. "If we were able at a given moment to be united to the very essence of God and to participate in it even in the very least degree, we should not at the moment be what we are, we should be God by nature" (Lossky, *Mystical Theology*, 69–70).

30. See ibid., 95.

being and constitute his energies. Supposedly, the Western view of divine ideas is static and indebted to Platonism, whereas the Eastern view offers a dynamic doctrine of divine ideas.[31] Lossky gives the following definition of divine energies in contrast to the divine essence:

> We are called to participate in the divine nature. We are therefore compelled to recognize in God an ineffable distinction, other than between His essence and His persons, according to which He is, under different aspects, both totally inaccessible and at the same time accessible. This distinction is that between the essence of God, or His nature, properly co-called [*sic.*], which is inaccessible, unknowable and incommunicable; and the energies or divine operations, forces proper to and inseparable from God's essence, in which He goes forth from Himself, manifests, communicates, and gives Himself.[32]

The majority of contemporary Eastern Orthodox theologians have adopted the distinction between essence and energies. The Neopalamite school, through the writings of Vladimir Lossky and Christos Yannaras, has brought this discussion to prominence in contemporary theological dialogue.[33] However, there are some figures, most notably John Zizioulas, who reject the distinction for other explanations of divine participation.

The convictions of the Palamite school arise from Pseudo-Dionysius. Dionysius argues that God, in his essence, is unknowable. There is no *analogia entis*, whereby one can view creation, and by expounding upon attributes of the created order, come to a valid explanation of God's nature. Rather, God is to be known by way of negation.[34] In apophatic theology, God is known in contrast

---

31. See the discussion of this in Finch, "Neo-Palamism," 237.

32. Lossky, *Mystical Theology*, 70.

33. See Russell's discussion of these figures in Russell, *Fellow Workers with God*, 134–42.

34. "Dionysius distinguishes two possible theological ways. One—that cataphatic or positive theology—proceeds by affirmations; the other—apophatic or negative theology—by negations. The first leads us to come knowledge of God, but is an imperfect way. The perfect way, the only way which is

to creation, rather than by and through creation in the manner Aquinas proposes.[35] As Staniloae explains:

> According to the patristic tradition, there is a rational or cataphatic knowledge of God, and an apophatic or ineffable knowledge. The latter is superior to the former because it completes it. God is not known in his essence, however, through either of these. We know God through cataphatic knowledge only as [the] creating and sustaining cause of the world, while through apophatic knowledge we gain a kind of direct experience of his mystical presence, which surpasses the simple knowledge of him as [the] cause who is invested with certain attributes similar to those of the world. This latter knowledge is termed apophatic because the mystical presence of God is experienced though it transcends the possibility of being defined by words. This knowledge is more adequate to God than is cataphatic knowledge.[36]

Though God is incomprehensible and unknowable according to his essence, God is genuinely revealed to creation. God is both absolutely transcendent and immanent with his creation, so that revelation and redemption are possible through God's energies. Coniaris purports:

> Divine energies are God Himself as He has manifested Himself to us. They are the ways by which God has come down to us and revealed Himself. Through His energies God continues to enter into relationship with people. By grace, that is by God's energies, we are no longer separated from God. His energies are the power of His grace which is experienced by believers today and is called theosis . . . Grace is understood by the Orthodox as the

---

fitting in regard to God, who is of His very nature unknowable, is the second—which leads us finally to total ignorance" (Lossky, *Mystical Theology*, 25).

35. "It is thus that St. Thomas Aquinas reduces the two ways of Dionysius into one, making a negative theology a corrective to affirmative theology. In attributing to God the perfections which we find in created beings, we must (according to St. Thomas) deny the mode according to which we understand these finite perfections" (ibid., 26).

36. Stăniloae, *Revelation and Knowledge*, 95.

energies of God in action, making God known and present to us.[37]

Inherent in Coniaris' definition is the conviction that grace is identified with God himself, rather than a created substance, as it is in Roman Catholic theology, or as the favor of God, as in Reformation theology. Roeber writes that:

> Grace, for the Orthodox, as it is among Lutherans, remains free, uncreated, beyond human control or manipulation, and to use a word that is foreign to Orthodox grammar but important to Lutherans—unmerited. But among the Orthodox, grace understood as "gift" actually is not merely passively "received." Rather, this is the Holy Spirit, whose active presence in the created world guarantees the continued presence of Christ and makes it possible for humans to respond to the offer, the response drawing the human person closer and closer toward union with God and effecting the transformation of the believer.[38]

Many Orthodox theologians fear that the Western emphasis on the fall and on the resulting loss of righteousness presumes a faulty ontology by which creation is cut off from God's being. For the Eastern Orthodox, union with God is a present reality and is inherent in creation prior to the eschaton. This union is the result of both God's energies and free human decision. To speak of grace as uncreated is to identify this union as present.[39] An analogy is often drawn between a sun and its rays. One does not have to experience the sun itself to know its effects. Heat and light are still felt, although only through the sun's rays rather than the celestial object itself. In the same way, God's energies are identified with God himself, yet are distinct from his essence.

37. Coniaris, *Achieving Your Potential*, 131.

38. Mattox and Roeber, *Changing Churches*, 81.

39. "For Palamas and, after him, Lossky and the neo-Palamites, this assertion was critical to avoid the conclusion many Western theologians had developed—namely, that the very life of God, or 'grace,' was 'created' and 'infused' in a fallen human nature, into a humanity cut off from real union with God since the Fall" (Mattox and Roeber, *Changing Churches*, 78–79).

This distinction is thoroughgoing in theological discussions for the East. Regarding the incarnation, for example, Lossky writes, "God condescends towards us 'in the energies' in which He is manifested; we mount towards Him in the 'unions' in which He remains incomprehensible by nature. The 'supreme theophany,' the perfect manifestation of God in the world by the incarnation of the Word, retains for us its apophatic character."[40] Thus, for Lossky, the essence and energies distinction is at work even in the event of the incarnation itself. Through the human nature of Christ, God shows himself to the world by manifesting his divine energies. However, even in Christ, God's essence remains hidden.

Two Kinds of Theosis

There are many different approaches to theosis in various authors and traditions, but there are two primary strands of thought on this subject. First, there is the earlier formulation as explained in Irenaeus and Athanasius. This approach to theosis is primarily theological in nature, arising from the teaching of the incarnation, and expounded upon through exegesis of biblical texts.[41] The second form is philosophical, taken from neoplatonism. This approach is represented in Pseudo-Dionysius, Clement of Alexandria, and Gregory Palamas. As Popov observes, "The starting point for the first was the deified flesh of Christ, while the starting point of the second was the Christian doctrine of God in its neoplatonic version."[42] Both of these perspectives are at work within Eastern Orthodox theology, but I propose that the first, rather than the second, is compatible with Lutheran soteriology.

---

40. Lossky, *Mystical Theology*, 39.

41. "The first orientation was rooted in the very depths of the popular faith, always positive and palpable; the second—which characterized the more educated theologians—was clothed in philosophical forms and did not reject the better aspects of neoplatonism, which in that epoch dominated all minds and attracted all hearts" (Popov, *Idea of Deification*, 44–45).

42. Ibid., 45.

What is problematic in the second approach is its cosmic dimension, which neglects the centrality of human salvation as well as its philosophical backing. Popov identifies this approach as the "idealist form" of deification. This has been promoted through Lossky's Neopalamite school as well as in the sophiology of Sergius Bulgakov, and has also been adopted in a modified form by contemporary Protestant theologians Jürgen Moltmann and Wolfhart Pannenberg. In the Neopalamite form, it is highly indebted to the work of Pseudo-Dionysius and Gregory Palamas. This approach "tends to see deification as the fulfillment in God not simply of humankind but of the entire created order."[43] Thus, the goal of theosis is not for individuals to participate in God through the incarnation, but is the deification of the cosmos.

In Lossky's approach, the deification of the cosmos was inherent in the mandate God gave to Adam. From creation, it was humanity's role to unite all things in Adam, to overcome division, and to deify creation. There are four steps to this deification. First, humankind would unite the sexes by living in chastity, thus the division within mankind itself would be overcome. Second, mankind would unite the garden of Eden—paradise—with the rest of creation. This would occur through "a love of God which would at once detach him from everything and allow him to embrace everything: always carrying Paradise in himself, he would have transformed the whole earth into paradise."[44] Humanity would unify the physical world through love, and eventually unify the spiritual and sensible worlds through angelic living. The final step is that "the cosmic Adam, by giving himself without return to God, would give Him back all His creation, and would receive from Him, by the mutuality of love, that is to say by grace, all that God possesses by virtue of His nature."[45] This would all finally result in "man's deification, and by him, of the whole universe."[46] God's plan

---

43. Russell, *Fellow Workers with God*, 47.
44. Lossky, *Orthodox Theology*, 74.
45. Ibid.
46. Ibid.

for redemption in the prelapsarian state was cosmic, for humanity and creation.

This cosmic plan was not abandoned after the fall, but was instead transferred from Adam, who failed in his task, to Christ, the second Adam. Lossky writes:

> The mission of the first Adam accordingly must be fulfilled by the celestial Adam, namely Christ . . . Thus, because of sin, in order that man might become God, it was necessary that God should become man, and that the second Adam should inaugurate the "new creation" in surmounting all the divisions of the old one. Indeed by His virginal birth, Christ overcomes the division of the sexes . . . On the cross Christ reunited the whole of the terrestrial cosmos to Paradise . . . After the Resurrection, the very body of Christ mocks spatial limitations, and in an integration of all that is sensible, unifies earth and heaven. By the Ascension, Christ reunites the celestial and terrestrial worlds, the angelical choirs to the human race. Finally, He who sits at the right hand of the Father introduces humanity above the angelic orders and into the Trinity itself; and these are the first fruits of cosmic deification.[47]

The work of Christ, in this approach, is not primarily for individuals, or even limited to the human race, but is instead about the deification of the universe.

Theosis as Christification

In certain strands of Eastern Orthodox soteriology, theosis is thoroughly grounded in the incarnation of the second person of the Holy Trinity. As Nellas argues, "Deification must not remain a general spiritual category but must acquire a specific anthropological content, which in the language of the Fathers means a content at once anthropological and christological: that is to say, it must be

---

47. Ibid., 75.

understood again as Christification."[48] This notion of Christification, as expounded upon by Nellas, exemplifies the patristic and biblical approach to soteriology that is so desperately needed in the contemporary church and which is commensurate with the Christocentric nature of Lutheran theology.

Nellas argues that all theology is related to Christology. The image of God in mankind, even in Gen 1, is in view of the incarnate Christ. Jesus is thus the archetypal man, in whom all of humanity participates and thus receives the divine image: "Christ constitutes the image of God and man the image of Christ; that is to say, that man is the image of the Image."[49] Like many Orthodox writers, Nellas purports that the *imago dei* is not related to mankind's static state, or mere attributes of the human nature, but to humanity's eschatological destiny.[50] He argues that "the greatness of man lies in his destiny, in his appointed end."[51] Humankind is created in the garden, not within a state of perfected righteousness, but as children with the ability to grow more fully into the image of God. The problem that exists between creature and creation does not exist only after the fall, but there is a great ontological chasm that needs to be bridged: "Prior to the hypostatic union of the divine nature with the human, man even before the fall was anterior to Christ, a fact which means that even then, in spite of not having sinned, man had need of salvation, since he was an imperfect and incomplete 'child.'"[52] Union with God was not inherent in humanity as created, but would grow as humanity developed. Sin put a barrier to Christification, and thus needed to be overcome through the cross and resurrection. Nellas writes:

> The Lord redeemed man from slavery to sin, death, and devil, but He also put into effect the work which had not

48. Nellas, *Deification in Christ*, 40.

49. Ibid., 24.

50. "It thus becomes clear that the essence of man is not found in the matter from which he was created but in the archetype on the basis of which he was formed and towards which he tends" (Nellas, *Deification in Christ*, 33).

51. Ibid., 30.

52. Ibid., 39.

been effected by Adam. He united him with God, granting him true "being" in God and raising him to a new creation. Christ accomplishes the salvation of man not only in a negative way, liberating him from the consequences of original sin, but also in a positive way, completing his iconic, prelapsarian "being." His relationship with man is not only that of healer. The salvation of man is something much wider than redemption; it coincides with deification.[53]

Nellas thus argues that salvation involves the removal of the negative aspects of the fall, but also includes humanity moving beyond the prelapsarian state into eschatological participation in God.

The fall created a situation in which humanity attempted to live autonomously, apart from God's life-giving grace.[54] Christ came to earth, incarnate by the Virgin Mary, for three primary reasons; he needed to overcome three "obstacles to the spiritual life: nature, sin, and death."[55] The incarnation solves the ontological problem. The natures of divinity and humanity are essentially at odds with one another. They are united in the person of Christ, bridging the metaphysical gap between Creator and creation: "With the birth of the 'blessed flesh' of the Lord the union was achieved of the two natures, the divine and the human, which until then had been 'separated' from one another."[56] Through the incarnation, Christ creates a new humanity and initiates an ontological change to creation.[57] The cross is Christ's means of defeating sin and evil. When Christ died on the

---

53. Ibid.

54. "The distance separating human nature from the divine took on tragic dimensions with the fall. In choosing to live, not with the life given to him by the breath of God, but in an autonomous way, man endowed sin with existence and life, although essentially it has no existence" (ibid., 110).

55. Ibid., 111.

56. Ibid.

57. "The hypostatic union recreates man, making his prelapsarian iconic being whole again. For this reason the conception by the Virgin Mary of the 'blessed flesh' of the Lord inaugurates a new human ontology, and Christ constitutes the real progenitor of a new humanity" (ibid., 112).

cross, sin and the devil, which had reigned over humanity, were defeated and destroyed. Finally, the resurrection solves the problem of death. Through Christ conquering death, humanity conquers death. Thus in the three acts of the incarnation, death, and resurrection of Christ, the human problems of nature, sin, and death are resolved.

Human participation in redemption occurs through participation in the person of Christ, primarily within the ecclesiastical community. Redemption is initially received by baptism, where the process of Christification begins:

> Through baptism, man's biological being actually participates in the death and resurrection of Christ. Baptism is literally a new birth in Christ and in this sense a new creation of man. This new creation, however, is not brought into existence *ex nihilo*, nor as in the case of the first man, out of pre-existing biological life, but out of the pre-existing biological being of man.[58]

Through this sacramental act, Christ's resurrection initiates the Christian's own resurrection through which the believer participates in the new humanity as a new creation. This act changes both the human person and human nature as Christ becomes "another self" to his people.[59] Through baptism, the Christian is united to Christ, forgiven of sin, and recreated. This, then, serves as the basis for Christification throughout life. Deification as a process is also a Eucharistic act. Through the Eucharist, "the union with Christ is complete and full."[60] Through partaking of Christ, his presence in the believer is strengthened, and an ontological act of renewal takes place. He transforms humanity to be like himself.

Overall, Nellas' proposal is attractive because he centers the idea of theosis around the person and work of Christ.[61] This

58. Ibid., 121.

59. Ibid., 124.

60. Ibid., 127.

61. I am by no means advocating a complete adoption of Nellas' theology of deification, which is still in many ways dependent on a purely Eastern understanding of theology in contradistinction to Lutheranism. This will become apparent later in the study.

Christological emphasis is in accordance with the earliest patristic and New Testament testimonies to the ontological change that occurs in the believer. According to Reformation thought, all blessings of God come through the reception of Christ and his benefits. In this framework, Christification can be adopted within Lutheran theology not as a replacement of forensic justification, but as a complementary teaching. Nellas' sacramental theology is also consistent with the sacramental theology of the Lutheran Church, which seeks commonality with the patristic teaching on baptism and the Supper.

Toward a Lutheran Synthesis

This chapter began with a Norman Russell's definition of the doctrine of theosis. A more precise proposed definition of Christification will help us to lay the groundwork for further discussion on this topic throughout the following chapters: Christification is the ontological union of God and man, initiated through the incarnation, which the Christian partakes in through faith. Through this union, that which belongs properly to Christ—namely divine incorruptibility and immortality—is transferred to the believer by faith. This union is increased and strengthened as the Christian participates in the sacramental life of the church, and it is demonstrated through growth in personal holiness.

It will be demonstrated that this Christological vision of deification is a thoroughly Pauline concept that is referenced in the Lutheran Confessions and developed in the later Lutheran tradition. Despite the lack of explicit "theosis" terminology, such ideas are indeed evident. This approach to theosis will also be shown to exist in the earliest writers of the church in opposition to the later approach to deification found in the works of such writers as Pseudo-Dionysius and Maximus the Confessor. The Apostolic Fathers, Irenaeus, Justin, and Athanasius, will be revealed to demonstrate that theosis, in its most ancient Christian form, is understood primarily as Christification, wherein Christians receive divine attributes through a participation in God that is initiated through the union of natures in the person of Christ.

2

Theosis in the Lutheran Tradition

THERE HAS BEEN A great deal of attention in recent years to the theme of deification in the writings of Luther, particularly in his 1535 Galatians commentary.[1] It has been argued that a doctrine of theosis is found in Luther that in many ways comports with that of the Eastern Orthodox tradition. While this study is important and there certainly is a doctrine of ontic-union with Christ and theosis throughout Luther's works, the present work will focus not on the corpus of Luther's own writings (as has been done elsewhere), but on the Confessions themselves. Many studies of Luther and theosis have proposed that there is a broad divergence between Luther and the Confessional tradition, thus giving Lutherans the option to follow either Luther's own theology or that of their Confessions.[2] Such a choice does not, however, need to be made because the Confessions themselves allow for and even teach a form of theosis. This concept of theosis is then expounded upon throughout the Lutheran dogmatic tradition, primarily under the rubric of "mystical union."

---

1. Luther, *LW* 26, 27. See also Mannermaa, *Christ Present in Faith*; Braaten and Jenson, *Union with Christ*; Kärkkäinen, *One with God*; Vainio, *Engaging Luther*; Mannermaa, *Two Kinds of Love*; Vainio, *Justification and Participation*; Schumacher, *"Who Do I Say That You Are?"* for a sampling of the scholarly discourse surrounding this issue.

2. "'Lutheran' has two meanings: it can denote either Martin Luther's theology as it is expressed in his own writings or the theology/theologies of the Lutheran confessions and subsequent Lutheran formulations. During the discussion I will show that these two have to be distinguished from each other" (Kärkkäinen, *One with God*, 37).

20

Luther's Confessional Writings

The Book of Concord contains three of Luther's own writings: the Small Catechism, the Large Catechism, and the Smalcald Articles. Though perhaps not as explicit as some of Luther's other works, there are hints of theosis in these documents that have gained Confessional status within the Lutheran tradition. Within Luther's writings, some prominent themes connected with theosis include participation in the divine life of the Holy Trinity, the contention that salvation involves a progressive element, and union with God through the sacramental life of the church.

For Luther, salvation is not a purely legal transaction divorced from participation in God. Rather, the purpose of salvation is not an isolated act of forgiveness, but to fellowship with God:

> For in all three articles God himself has revealed and opened to us the most profound depths of his fatherly heart and his pure, unutterable love. For this very purpose he created us, so that he might redeem us and make us holy, and, moreover, having granted and bestowed upon us everything in heaven and on earth, he has also given us his Son and his Holy Spirit, through whom he brings us to himself. (LC II.64)

In Luther's view, God's self-giving in Christ is essential to God's own character. All three articles of the creed, which are focused on God's act of redemption, don't just demonstrate something *about* God, but in fact reveal his *identity* as one who redeems out of his fatherly love.[3] God donates his own self to the Christian believer out of his selfless character.[4] The believer then receives from God everything in heaven and on earth, which ultimately involves the reception of the Son and the Holy Spirit. This

---

3. Gorman has noted this in Paul's theology. He calls Phil 2:6–11 Paul's "master story," which summarizes his primary theological concerns. The nature of Christ's humiliation is not opposed to the ordinary way God works, but is in fact the essence of who God is. God is acting as Lord when he is a servant (Gorman, *Inhabiting the Cruciform God*, 9–39).

4. See Kilcrease, *Self Donation of God*.

culminates in a union with all three persons of the Holy Trinity. Luther expounds on his meaning further in this article, stating:

> But the Creed brings pure grace and makes us righteous and acceptable to God. Through this knowledge we come to love and delight in all the commandments of God because we see here in the Creed how God gives himself completely to us, with all his gifts and power, to help us keep the Ten Commandments: the Father gives us all creation, Christ all his works, the Holy Spirit all his gifts. (LC II.68)

This statement points to Luther's thoroughgoing Trinitarianism. The gifts given in the gospel are through each person of the Holy Trinity. The one who believes receives creation, the works of Christ, and the blessings of the Holy Spirit as divine gifts. Note, however, that Luther does not only speak of the gifts of the Holy Trinity being given in faith, but also *God himself.*[5] He writes that "God gives himself completely to us, with all his gifts and power." Thus divine gifts are not separate from the divine being. God gives himself to believers, and through that gift of himself, the Christian receives God's blessings. Luther does not fall into the false dichotomy espoused by much of the Post-Reformation church, which divorces God from his gifts by arguing that Christ's righteousness is imputed apart from his person. Grace, while encapsulating the notion of unmerited favor, is connected to God's being. Grace includes the presence of God himself, through which unmerited gifts and favor are granted to the recipient.

As demonstrated above, Luther does not speak of salvation purely in forensic terms. While forensic justification is an essential aspect of Luther's theology, this is not taught at the expense of any element of progressive holiness. Union with God initiates a process wherein the Christian obeys God's commandments and ceases from sin. Despite arguments to the contrary, there is a third use of the law in Luther's teaching, which appears in the Large Catechism.[6] After

---

5. As Mannermaa points out, Christ is both favor and gift (Mannermaa, *Christ Present in Faith*, 19–21).

6. Engelbrecht has recently done a monumental study on the issue of

giving a lengthy exposition on each of the Ten Commandments, Luther gives the following summary:

> Here, then, we have the Ten Commandments, a summary of divine teaching on what we are to do to make our whole life pleasing to God. They are the true fountain from which all good works must spring, the true channel through which all good works must flow. Apart from these Ten Commandments no action or life can be good or pleasing to God, no matter how great or precious it may be in the eyes of the world. (LC I.311)

The commandments don't serve a purely negative function in Luther's theology. They do always expose sin, pointing to Christ as the one who takes away sin, but there still is a place for using the law as a guide for good works.[7] An important distinction must be made here between the Lutheran and Orthodox view of synergy in relation to the process of deification. For Luther, the law can never sanctify. The law can show what a good work is, but does not give the power to do such works. Following Augustine's treatise, "The Spirit and the Letter,"[8] Luther argues that the power to obey God's commands always arises through the gospel. The act of divine forgiveness grants the power to obey the law. Luther writes that the Holy Spirit "daily increase[s] holiness on earth through these two means, the Christian church and the forgiveness of sins" (LC II.59). The theotic movement toward God is not due to Christians' obedience, but continual reception of the forgiveness of sins, especially as granted through the sacraments. In contrast to this idea, in the Eastern Orthodox view, both God's grace given in the sacraments *and* human obedience to the Ten Commandments are means of sanctification.[9]

Luther and the third use in which he convincingly demonstrates that a third use does exist in Luther's theology See Engelbrecht, *Friends of the Law*.

7. And thus, the *lex semper accusat* principle of Melanchthon still holds within a third use framework. See Apol IX.38.

8. *Spir. et litt.*, NPNF1 5:80–115.

9. "In addition to repentance, we grow toward theosis by keeping the commandments" (Coniaris, *Achieving Your Potential*, 91).

Luther confesses that "holiness has begun and is growing daily" (LC II.57) in the faithful Christian, but acknowledges that only eschatologically "our flesh will be put to death, will be buried with all its uncleanness, and will come forth gloriously and arise to complete and perfect holiness in a new, eternal life" (LC II.57). Perfectionism is expressly denied, since in this life the Christian is always *simul iustus et peccator*. Yet, the *simul* does not refer *exclusively* to total states. There is also a sense in which the believer is partially righteous and partially sinful, wherein the flesh is put to death as the new man rises to life. Not only are we imputed righteous by faith, but also, "we receive a different, new, clean heart and that, for the sake of Christ our mediator, God will and does regard us as completely righteous and holy" (SA XIII.1). Thus, imputation of righteousness coexists with the impartation of holiness, which grows daily.

Luther's theology of deification is thoroughly grounded within his baptismal theology. In his explanation of the first petition of the Lord's Prayer, Luther writes:

> But what is it to pray that his name may become holy? Is it not already holy? Answer: Yes, in its essence it is always holy, but our use of it is not holy. God's name was given to us when we became Christians and were baptized, and so we are called children of God and have the sacraments, through which he incorporates us into himself with the result that everything that is God's must serve for our use. (LC III.37)

Christian holiness is grounded in God's own holiness, which is received in the waters of baptism. Through baptism, one becomes a Christian and is incorporated into God. This is a clear expression of participation in divinity that is fully compatible with the Athanasian view of theosis.

In Luther's view, baptism is a divine work: "To be baptized in God's name is to be baptized not by human beings but by God himself. Although it is performed by human hands, it is nevertheless truly God's own act" (LC IV.10). It is God who both initiates baptism, working through the hands of the baptizer, and who is received at baptism. Luther enumerates a number of blessings that are received by the Christian through the baptismal act. Baptism brings soteriological blessings such as deliverance from sin and immortality, freedom from the devil, and entrance into the kingdom of God.[10] In Luther's theology, baptism is a divine work of grace, not a human action, and thus deepens the doctrine of *sola gratia* rather than obscuring it.[11] Since Christ's benefits are not separated from his person in Luther's theology, baptism involves a reception of the Holy Trinity rather than the gifts of God alone: "Christians always have enough to do to believe what baptism promises and brings—victory over death and the devil, forgiveness of sin, God's grace, the entire Christ, and the Holy Spirit with his gifts" (LC IV.41). Luther purports that it is the "whole Christ" that is received at baptism, along with the Holy Spirit. Under this approach, baptism in fact initiates the process of theosis, because through baptism, the new Christian receives the indwelling Christ and the Holy Spirit. This makes the Christian a new creature and gives the freedom of will to seek out the good.

Baptism, for Luther, is not simply a one-time act, but is valid throughout the individual Christian's existence. In baptism, the old self is destroyed, and the new self is raised. Eschatological existence through participation in Christ begins, for as Luther explains:

> These two parts, being dipped under the water and emerging from it, point to the power and effect of

10. "This is the simplest way to put it: the power, effect, benefit, fruit, and purpose of baptism is that it saves. For no one is baptized in order to become a prince, but, as the words say, 'to be saved.' To be saved, as everyone well knows, is nothing else than to be delivered from sin, death, and the devil, to enter into Christ's kingdom, and to live with him forever" (LC IV.24–25).

11. "Yes it is true that our works are of no use for salvation. Baptism, however, is not our work, but God's work (for, as was said, you must distinguish Christ's baptism quite clearly from a bath-keeper's baptism). God's works are salutary and necessary for salvation . . . Thus you see plainly that baptism is not a work that we do but that it is a treasure that God gives us and faith grasps" (LC IV.35–36).

> baptism, which is nothing else than the slaying of the old Adam and the resurrection of the new creature, both of which must continue in us our whole life long. Thus a Christian life is nothing else than a daily baptism, begun once and continuing ever after. For we must keep at it without ceasing, always purging whatever pertains to the old Adam, so that whatever belongs to the new creature may come forth . . . Now, when we enter Christ's kingdom, this corruption must daily decrease so that the longer we live the more gentle, patient, and meek we become, and the more we break away from greed, hatred, envy, and pride. (LC IV.65–67)

Baptism is part of the process of salvation by which the individual's sinful nature is put to death and the Christian comes to obey God's commandments through the indwelling Christ. This becomes a daily reality as sin is decreased and righteousness increased with each passing each day. It is baptism that grants the power of Christification, wherein the Christian is continually brought to conform to the image of the indwelling Savior through participation in him through faith.[12]

There is also a Eucharistic element to theosis within the theology of Luther. Under his realist view of the sacrament, Luther contends, "in this sacrament he [Jesus] offers us all the treasures he brought from heaven for us, to which he most graciously invites us" (LC V.66). The primary blessing given in the sacrament is the forgiveness of sins, which comes through the reception of Christ's body and blood. However, the sacrament also strengthens the Christian to do God-pleasing works:

> Therefore, it is appropriately called food for the soul, for it nourishes and strengthens the new creature. For in the first instance, we are born anew through baptism. However, our human flesh and blood, as I have said, have not lost their old skin. There are so many hindrances and attacks of the devil and the world that we often grow weary

---

12. Baptism is also a Pneumatological reality: "In baptism we are given the grace, Spirit, and strength to suppress the old creature so that the new may come forth and grow strong" (LC IV.76).

and faint and at times even stumble. Therefore the Lord's Supper is given as a daily food and sustenance so that our faith may be refreshed and strengthened and that it may not succumb in the struggle but become stronger and stronger. For the new life should be one that continually develops and progresses. (LC V.23–25)

Thus, the Lord's Supper is given both for the forgiveness of sins and for protection against sin, so that the Christian might progress in holiness and flee from the devil.

In the Large Catechism, Luther teaches a doctrine of theosis, although without using that exact terminology. Luther describes the Christian life as a process of becoming holy, although he acknowledges that Christians will always struggle with sin. Justification—the forgiveness of sins—is always in view for Luther, but not to the neglect of concern for personal holiness. In Luther's works we also find a sense of a real-ontic union with God. This union is given in baptism, received through faith, and strengthened by the Eucharist.

The Apology of the Augsburg Confession

Though not as explicit as Luther himself, Melanchthon includes certain themes in the Apology of the Augsburg Confession that comport with a teaching of theosis. Melanchthon is careful to use both forensic and participationist language when discussing soteriological themes. He writes,

> Instead, we maintain that, properly and truly, by faith itself we are regarded as righteous for Christ's sake, that is, we are acceptable to God. And because "to be justified" means that out of unrighteous people righteous people are made or regenerated, it also means that they are pronounced or regarded as righteous. For Scripture speaks both ways. Accordingly, we first want to show that faith alone makes a righteous person out of an unrighteous one, that is, it alone receives the forgiveness of sins. (Apol IV.72)

Justification is a forensic reality, for it not only includes the imputation of Christ's righteousness, but is also synonymous with regeneration. Through faith, the Christian is both imputed righteous and made righteous. Faith both "receives the forgiveness of sins, justifies us, and makes alive" (Apol IV.62). Spiritual life begins through justification, because justification is "the making of a righteous person out of an unrighteous one or as regeneration" (Apol IV.78). Regeneration includes the reception of God, and new spiritual impulses within someone's heart.[13]

Melanchthon also argues that salvation includes a lifelong process of holy living. Through the reception of Christ and the Holy Spirit, "the keeping of the law must begin in us and then increase more and more. And we include both simultaneously, namely, the inner spiritual impulses and the outward good works" (Apol IV.136). In opposition to the alleged antimonianism of the Lutheran Church, the Reformer makes it apparent that Christians do indeed obey God's law, although they are still burdened by sin. By faith, God "makes a righteous person out of an unrighteous one" (Apol IV.150), and thus, through faith, the law can begin to be kept.[14]

The Osiandrian Controversy

After the death of Martin Luther, a number of controversies arose within the Lutheran branch of the Reformation. Through these controversies, positions on various issues were clarified with the writing of the Formula of Concord. Especially important for the present study is the controversy surrounding the teachings of Andreas Osiander, who argued that Luther's doctrine of justification is not forensic, but rather centers around the indwelling of Christ's divine nature.[15] According to Osiander, there is a broad diver-

13. "Because faith truly brings the Holy Spirit and produces a new life in our hearts, it must also produce spiritual impulses in our hearts" (Apol IV.125).

14. This is not optional for the believer, but "Since this faith is a new life, it necessarily produces new impulses and new works" (Apol IV.250).

15. On this controversy, see Arand et al., *Lutheran Confessions*, 217–26; Preus and Rosin, *Contemporary Look*, 137–62.

gence between redemption and justification. Redemption occurs through the death and resurrection of Christ as historical realities. Justification, however, is separate from this; in justification, the Christian is righteous because of the indwelling of Christ's divine nature. Osiander soon became the subject of controversy, for he failed to emphasize the objective work of Christ's death and resurrection in his discussions of the righteousness that avails before God, thereby causing Lutherans to wonder whether Osiander had essentially adopted the uncertainty of salvation inherent in the medieval system that Luther had sought to overthrow. The authors of the Formula rejected Osiandrianism because:

> . . . it operated on a false metaphysical base that denied that God changes reality through his Word of forgiveness. It viewed the gift of God's grace as something quasi-substantial, within the human creature, rather than as the restoration of humanity to sinners through the transformation of the relationship between them and God.[16]

This neoplatonic metaphysical conviction, which operated apart from Luther's Word-centric theology, caused the Concordists to reject Osiander's proposal as inherently opposed to a Reformation understanding of *sola fide*.

This controversy is particularly important because opponents of the Finnish school of Luther interpretation have argued that contemporary theologians who read theosis in Luther are essentially guilty of the Osiandrian error.[17] It is argued that what is rejected by the Formula is a doctrine of justification that is participationist, and thus most participationist soteriological schemes are inherently anti-Confessional. This has not been helped by the fact that Tuomo Mannermaa argues for such a divergence between the theology of Luther and the Formula of Concord: "This dis-

---

16. Arand et al., *Lutheran Confessions*, 225.

17. Schumacher claims that "despite his criticism of Osiander for separating the two natures in Christ's person and deriving the Christian's righteousness exclusively from union with the divine nature, Peura seems to fall prey to exactly the same error. Here again he follows Mannermaa" (Schumacher, *"Who Do I Say That You Are?"* 83).

crepancy between the view of the FC and the position of Luther makes one wonder which view actually represents 'the Lutheran' understanding of this doctrine."[18] Thus, it is proposed that we must choose between the theology of Luther and that of the Lutheran Confessions.

I propose, in contrast to the common contention made by both proponents and critics of the Finnish school of thought, that the Formula does not condemn what Mannermaa proposes as Luther's teaching on mystical union.[19] What the Concordists condemn in the teaching of Osiander is that the individual is justified based on the indwelling divine nature of Christ. Contrary to this, Luther teaches that justification comes as a result of both natures of Christ, and primarily through his life-giving death and resurrection. There is no opposition between the objective acts of Christ's life and the gifts given through indwelling in Luther's thought, as there is in Osiander's theology.[20] The primary concern of the Formula, in arguing against Osiander, is to offer a defense of salvation by grace. This is why the majority of Article III argues not against mystical union, but against the contention that justification is based on the renewal or good works of the sinner. For example:

> Therefore, even if the converted and believers have the beginnings of renewal, sanctification, love, virtues, and good works, yet these cannot, should not, and must not be introduced or mixed with the article of justification before God, so that the proper honor may be accorded to our Redeemer Christ and (because our new obedience is imperfect and impure) so that the consciences under attack may have a reliable comfort. (FC SD III.35)

The point here is that justification is not based on infused love, virtues, or good works inherent in the believer. It may be

---

18. Mannermaa, *Christ Present in Faith*, 5.

19. Kurt Marquart makes the same argument in Marquart, "Luther and Theosis," 182–205.

20. This is especially the case in Osiander's unwarrented division between redemption and justification.

argued, however, that according to the Formula, mystical union is always a result of justification rather than a prior or simultaneous reality: "this indwelling is a result of the righteousness of faith which precedes it" (FC SD III.54). Note that what is rejected here is the idea that *this* indwelling is a result of justification. It is rejected that the Osiandrian sense of indwelling—the infusion of virtues and love—precedes faith, because this would result in a righteousness based on works.[21] That doesn't mean that the indwelling of the person of Christ in faith must be subsequent to justification. It does not deny that Christ gives his whole person to the believer in justification. In fact, the Confessions reject the notion that "not God but only the gifts of God dwell in believers." (FC SD III.65)

It is worth noting that the Article III of the Formula says, "For any further, necessary explanation of this lofty and sublime article on justification before God, upon which the salvation of our souls depends, we wish to recommend to everyone the wonderful, magnificent exposition by Dr. Luther of St. Paul's Epistle to the Galatians, and for the sake of brevity we refer to it at this point" (FC SD III.67). This gives the Galatians commentary a semi-Confessional status, since the Lutheran fathers agreed unanimously to point to this text as a correct exposition to justification. It is the Galatians commentary of Luther that has, in fact, served as the basis for the Finnish school of thought. In a careful reading of Luther's Galatians commentary, it seems undeniable that Christ is present in faith, and that justification involves the reception of Christ's person as righteousness. For example:

21. As Marquart observes: "The following error is rejected and condemned: 'That faith does not look solely to the obedience of Christ, but also to his divine nature in so far as it dwells and works within us, and that by such indwelling our sins are covered up in the sight of God.' What is rejected is not that in 'faith itself Christ is present,' but that faith looks 'also to his divine nature in so far as it dwells and works in us' for justification. In other words, in so far as faith produces inner renewal or sanctification. It is a question of 'this indwelling' or 'such indwelling,' that is, Osiander's sort of 'indwelling of God's essential righteousness' that is rejected. Luther's *in ipsa fide Christus adest* 'in faith itself Christ is present' is quite untouched by the rejection of Osiander's fancies" (Marquart, "Luther and Theosis," 201).

> But so far as justification is concerned, Christ and I must
> be so closely attached that He lives in me and I in Him.
> What a marvelous way of speaking! Because He lives in
> me, whatever grace, righteousness, life, peace, and salva-
> tion there is in me is all Christ's; nevertheless, it is mine as
> well, by the cementing and attachment that are through
> faith, by which we become as one body in the Spirit.[22]

Luther argues for a great exchange between Christ and the
believer, wherein Christ gives his own person to the believer as he
is grasped by faith. Through this union, divine qualities are transferred to the believer.[23]

With this being said, there are certain themes in the Formula
that point to a form of theosis that is consistent with the theology
of Luther and the early fathers. First is the Formula's contention
that salvation includes a process of becoming righteous. Alhough
apart from grace, the will is in bondage to sin, it is confessed that
through the renewed will, we receive "the gifts of the Holy Spirit,
which cleanses human beings and daily makes them more upright
and holier" (FC SD II.35). Sanctification, according to the authors
of the Formula, is a process that occurs through the indwelling of
God, particularly the Holy Spirit. This is a process wherein people
are gradually made holier. This is not an individualistic enterprise,
but "through the ministry of preaching [the Holy Spirit] brings
us into the Christian community, in which he sanctifies us and
brings about in us a daily increase in good works" (FC SD II.38).
This progress comes through both inner renewal and the outward
display of good works. The concept of synergy is also confessed,
though qualified so as to emphasize the work of God within the
believer: "as soon as the Holy Spirit has begun his work of rebirth
and renewal in us through the Word and the holy sacraments,
it is certain that on the basis of his power we can and should be
cooperating with him, though still in great weakness" (FC SD
II.65). There are some common themes between the Lutheran and

22. Luther, *LW* 26:167–68.

23. This commentary is expounded upon elsewhere; see Mannermaa,
Christ Present in Faith.

Eastern Orthodox view on this topic. Both traditions confess that believers must obey God's law, and are given the ability to do so through the indwelling Spirit. Both traditions allow for some type of synergy in the process of becoming holy. There is an important divergence here, however, between the Lutheran Reformers and the Eastern Church. According to Luther and the Concordists, whatever cooperation the Christian has with God's grace is minimal. For Lutherans, the work of salvation is monergistic; election, rebirth, faith, and perseverance are acts of God granted by grace. The Christian can and does cooperate with God in the realm of good works, but God's grace takes primacy such that "if God could withdraw his gracious hand from such people, they could not for one moment remain obedient to God" (FC SD II.66). Thus, the emphasis of the Eastern fathers on the freedom of the human will is incompatible with Luther's thoroughgoing monergism.[24]

Article III of the Formula of Concord addresses Osiander's errors. In doing so, the Concordists clearly emphasize the truth latent in Osiander's flawed approach to justification. The Formula proposes that righteousness is imputed by faith. This act of justification is not simply the imputation of righteousness and the forgiveness of sins, but also involves the adoption of the Christian as well as the reception of eschatological life.[25] It is a death and resurrection.[26] Though the act of imputation is distinct from good works, a life of virtue is a necessary aspect of redemption: "The Holy Spirit is given to those who, as has been said, are righteous before God (that is, have been received into grace) . . . He renews

24. This can be traced back to the Semipelagian controversy between John Cassian and Prosper of Aquitaine. The Eastern Church has adopted Cassian's approach to the fall, which argues that the will is not in bondage in the post-lapsarian state, though still damaged. The Lutheran church has adopted Prosper's moderate Augustinianism, which emphasizes the priority of God's grace over human will and God's unconditional act of election.

25. "Poor sinful people are justified before God, that is, absolved—pronounced free of all sins and of the judgment of the damnation that they deserved and accepted as children and heirs of eternal life" (FC SD III.20).

26. "For when the human being is justified through faith (which the Holy Spirit alone bestows), it is truly a rebirth, because a child of wrath becomes a child of God and is therefore brought from death to life" (ibid.).

them and sanctifies them, and he creates in them love toward God and the neighbor" (FC SD III.23). Sanctification is a result of justification, as the Spirit is given to dwell in the believer.[27] It is confessed that "once people are justified, the Holy Spirit also renews and sanctified them. From this renewal and sanctification the fruits of good works follow" (FC SD III.41). Distinction is made between a "dead faith," which demonstrates its falsehood by lacking good works, and a living, real, and active justifying faith which always results in new obedience. Finally, it is confessed that there is a real union with the Holy Trinity that occurs through faith:

> To be sure, God the Father, Son and Holy Spirit, who is the eternal and essential righteousness, dwells through faith in the elect, who have become righteous through Christ and are reconciled with God. (For all Christians are temples of God the Father, Son, and Holy Spirit, who moves them to act properly.) (FC SD III.54)

With these words, it is confessed that there is a true union with the divine nature that a believer receives through faith. This is a Trinitarian reality, wherein the believer is indwelt by the Trinitarian persons, who act within the believer. This is a clear testimony to a belief in a form of theosis among the Lutheran Reformers.

Mystical Union in Lutheran Orthodoxy

Though Luther's emphasis on ontological union with God is not as pronounced in the works of later Lutheran writers, there is a clear confession of a mystical union which did not appear in the Reformed Scholastics. For our purposes, two writers will be examined: Adolf Hoenecke and Heinrich Schmid. Hoenecke, an influential nineteenth-century American theologian, wrote in the Lutheran Scholastic tradition and had a profound impact on

---

27. "Likewise, too, although renewal and sanctification are a blessing of our mediator Christ and a work of the Holy Spirit, they do not belong in the article or in the treatment of justification before God but rather result from it since, because of our corrupted flesh, they are never fully pure and perfect in this life" (FC SD III.28).

American Lutheranism, especially in the Wisconsin Synod. Hoenecke is particularly useful because his work serves as a concise summary of the seventeenth century's theological tradition, for he cites the most influential Lutheran dogmaticians of the late sixteenth through early eighteenth centuries to validate his work. Hoenecke speaks of mystical union much more extensively than other standard dogmatic texts of that period, including such works as Francis Pieper's *Christian Dogmatics*. Schmid's work likewise offers a summary of the Lutheran Scholastic tradition, for he compiles quotes from various seventeenth- and eighteenth-century writers on a variety of topics. Schmid also discusses mystical union in some detail.

Adolf Hoenecke

Hoenecke writes in typical Scholastic fashion, writing on various theological loci by Scriptural defense, an overview of criticisms, and a consequent refutation of such criticisms. He places mystical union within the discussion of the *ordo salutis*. For Hoenecke there is a logical order of God's redemptive acts as applied to the individual. In this scheme, mystical union with God follows God's gracious act of justification. Hoenecke defines the *unione mystica* in the following manner:

> The mystical union of the believers with God consists in that the triune God through the Holy Spirit essentially is graciously present in believers, through which those thus united with God not only blessedly rejoice and are filled with comfort and peace but are also made constantly more certain in grace, strengthened in sanctification, and preserved for eternal life.[28]

Hoenecke notes that this doctrine is consistently taught in the Lutheran tradition, but is expounded upon more fully by the later dogmaticians. This union can be labeled as a spiritual union, mystical union, or even substantial union with God "because it is

---

28. Hoenecke, *Evangelical Lutheran Dogmatics*, 3:385.

the union of two substances, God and man."[29] This union occurs through faith, wherein God indwells the heart of the Christian. Hoenecke argues against Ritschl's notion[30] of mystical union in writing, "These names are more than figurative terms, more than names of a merely moral unity of the human will with the divine will or of a merely divine influence through external means."[31] Like Mannermaa, Hoenecke argues for a real substantial union, rather than a union of will or purpose.

Hoenecke's formulation of mystical union is identical in many ways to the Eastern Orthodox approach to theosis. He writes,

> According to these passages the essence of the mystical union is that God, according to his substance, in a miraculous way is close to the substance of humans and permeates their substance with his essence (John 17:21–23), and dwelling in the believers, he so works in them that they are filled with knowledge and all the fullness of God (Eph 3:17–19). When we describe the mystical union as the presence of the divine substance with the substance of humans, we express its intimacy. Two intimate friends cannot be so closely united. With the substance of their souls they are near each other; but God and the believers are in each other. The substance of both touches each other most closely; indeed the divine permeates the human. But self-evidently, every thought of an essential partaking of the believer in the substance of God, every mixing of God and man, every pantheistic notion of deification is far from this.[32]

This union of persons could accurately be described as a real-ontic union. Divinity indwells humanity. Hoenecke even goes so far as to say that the human is permeated with the divine essence, though he is willing to qualify this statement by rejecting "an essential partaking of the believer in the substance of God." Thus,

29. Ibid.

30. Ritschl argued that union with Christ was simply a union of wills, with no ontological participation.

31. Hoenecke, *Evangelical Lutheran Dogmatics*, 3:386.

32. Ibid.

Hoenecke guards against apotheosis. He does not, however, see the necessity of making a distinction between God's essence and energies. This union is a union of two substances, not of the human essence and divine energies. In some sense, this goes farther than the Eastern view of theosis in purporting that the divine substance permeates the human.

Heinrich Schmid

Like Hoenecke, Schmid places mystical union within the *ordo salutis*. This event occurs "at the moment when man is justified and regenerated."[33] He argues against a figurative or metaphorical interpretation of union, and also rejects the idea that God's union with man is simply the bestowal of divine gifts through the Holy Spirit. Instead, it is "the union of the substance of God with the substance of man, in consequence of which God pours out the fullness of his gracious gifts upon the regenerate."[34] Although God, in some sense, dwells in all of creation, he is present in believers in a "special sense."[35] Schmid is also clear to avoid any sense of apotheosis, thus defending the Creator/creature distinction. He writes:

> As we are unable to give a more specific representation of the nature and manner of this union, we limit ourselves to the removal of erroneous views of it. It would be wrong to suppose that in this union the two substances, the divine and the human, are united in such a manner that the two substances become one, or that the one is absorbed in the other; or, as if out of the two persons, God and man, one person would be constituted, as in the case of the two natures in Christ. The mystical union is therefore not a substantial and not a personal union.[36]

33. Schmid, *Doctrinal Theology*, 495.
34. Ibid., 496.
35. Ibid.
36. Ibid.

Schmid does not see a need to make a distinction between energies and essence in God, but is content to argue that there is no absorption of one substance into the other. This leaves the mystery of union to stand without any particular explanation of how it occurs. Like the Chalcedonian definition of the union of two natures, the Lutheran Scholastics were willing to affirm the concept of mystical union by way of negation, without giving a positive explanation of the manner in which this mystery functions.

Johannes Andreas Quenstedt explains this union by way of negating various possible approaches to this subject. He rejects any sense of transubstantiation, or "the conversion of our substance into the substance of God and of Christ."[37] Continuing his Eucharistic metaphors, Quenstedt also rejects consubstantiation, or "that of two united essences there is formed one substance."[38] Schmid explains why there is no confusion of essences in the *unione mystica*, writing: "The mystical union is, therefore, indeed called a union of substances, but strictly taken, not a formal substantial union (such as is that of a graft which coalesces with the trunk into the essence of the tree numerically one), but it is an accidental union."[39] This assures that believers maintain their own identity, and are not absorbed into God. Humans retain their humanity and essential createdness, while participating in God's substance by grace.

There is, in some writings, an explicit confession that the human person partakes in the divine essence. Quenstedt purports that "through a special approximation of [God's] essence, and by a gracious operation, he is in them, just as also believers are in him."[40] Christians do not become divine through a confusion of two essences; they remain human creatures while being incorporated into God's own life, partaking of his essence. This union is Trinitarian,[41] but has a specific Christological focus. Quenstedt

---

37. Quenstedt, quoted in ibid., 501.

38. Ibid.

39. Ibid.

40. Ibid., 498.

41. "The mystical union is the real and most intimate conjunction of the

confesses that this union is "a true and real and most intimate conjunction of the divine and human nature of the theanthropic Christ with a regenerated man."[42] This union is effected by means of Word and Sacrament, wherein Christ and his benefits are received.[43] The Scholastics often used the imagery of marriage to express this mystical union. As Calov argues:

> The espousal of Christ with believers is that by which he eternally marries himself to believers through faith, so that they become one spirit, and by his power communicates to them, as to his spiritual bride, intimate and enduring love, all his blessings and all his glory, so as finally to lead them to his bed, and cohabit with them in his celestial and eternal kingdom.[44]

This concept is defended by Schmid, who cites the marriage metaphor used in the book of Hosea[45] as well as Paul's statements regarding marriage in Eph 5.[46]

There is some disagreement among Scholastic theologians as to the priority of mystical union and justification in the *ordo salutis*. The Finnish school of Luther interpretation has argued that mystical union precedes justification in Luther's theology, meaning that Christ's benefits cannot be received apart from Christ's person. This interpretation has been followed by Kurt Marquart[47] and

---

substance of the Sacred Trinity and the God-man Christ" (ibid.).

42. Ibid.

43. "The mystical union of Christ with the believer is a true and real and most intimate conjunction of the divine and human nature of the theanthropic Christ with a regenerated man, which is effected by the virtue of the merit of Christ through the Word and Sacraments; so that Christ constitutes a spiritual unit with the regenerated person, and operates in him and through him, and those things which the believer does or suffers he appropriates to himself, so that the man does not live, as to his spiritual and divine life, of himself, but by the faith of the Son of God, until he is taken to heaven" (ibid.).

44. Ibid.

45. "And I will betroth you to me forever. I will betroth you to me in righteousness and in justice, in steadfast love and in mercy" (Hos 2:19).

46. "This mystery is profound, and I am saying that it refers to Christ and the church" (Eph 5:32).

47. Marquart, "Luther and Theosis."

myself as well.[48] Others have stated that the Formula of Concord necessitates the logical priority of justification over mystical union in its rejection of Osiandrianism. Schmid demonstrates that both of these positions have been taken within the Lutheran Scholastic tradition. Indeed, Quenstedt is quoted as saying: "according to our mode of conceiving of them, justification and regeneration are prior in order to the mystical union. For when, in regeneration, a man receives faith, and by faith is justified, then only he begins to be mystically united to God."[49] In this perspective, mystical union necessarily follows justification. However, other theologians have argued the opposite. Hollaz states:

> Although the mystical union, by which God dwells in the soul as in a temple, may, according to our mode of conception, follow justification in the order of nature, it is however to be acknowledged that the formal union of faith, by which Christ is apprehended, put on, and united with us, as a mediator and the author of grace and pardon, logically precedes justification. For faith is imputed for righteousness, so far as this receives the merit of Christ, and so unites it with ourselves as to make it ours.[50]

The primary point in Hollaz' formulation is that we must be united with Christ in order to receive his benefits. One must be united with Christ and his merit in order for that merit to be imputed to the believer for righteousness. If union is divided into two distinct stages, then the Osiandrian error can be guarded against, even as Hollaz' and Mannermaa's concerns are validated. There is the union of Christ, wherein Christ is present in faith, granting his benefits subjectively to the recipient. It is in this sense that union precedes justification. However, growth in one's union with God, wherein moral qualities are given to the believer, follows rather than precedes the act of justification inasmuch as sanctification is a result of justification. In this way, Luther is correct in arguing for Christ's presence in faith (the first kind of union) that receives

48. Cooper, *Righteousness of One*, 40–67.
49. Schmid, *Doctrinal Theology*, 496.
50. Ibid., 497.

justification, and the Formula is correct in placing union as a result (the second kind of union), rather than cause, of justification.

Sanctification in the Lutheran Tradition

Along with mystical union, the Lutheran tradition has claimed that there is an ongoing process wherein the believer becomes holy, being gradually renewed in the image of God. This is referred to as "sanctification" or "renovation," which is a work of God following justification. The term "sanctification" has both a narrow sense and a broad sense. In the broad sense, sanctification refers to the full economy of salvation, including: "the bestowal of faith, justification, sanctification as the inner transformation of man, perseverance in the faith, and the complete renewal on Judgment Day."[51] This broad sense is used to underscore the fact that Scripture most often speaks of sanctification as an event that is synonymous with justification.[52] However, theologians have utilized the term primarily in the narrow sense, to refer to "that activity of the appropriating grace of the Holy Spirit by virtue of which the justified person day by day lays aside the sinful nature still clinging to him."[53] This narrow approach to sanctification demonstrates that growth in holiness and renewal in the image of God is essential to Lutheran soteriology.

Justification is a more central soteriological category than sanctification. This is because justification, rather than

51. Pieper, *Christian Dogmatics*, 3:3.

52. Voigt rightly states, "In the New Testament use of the term sanctification does not mean a progress in holiness, much less a progress into holiness" (Voigt, *Biblical Dogmatics*, 183). Yet, Voigt also confesses that "what is meant by sanctification, as the word is commonly used" is "altogether Scriptural. Progress in holy living is taught in all that is said in the Scriptures of the conflict of the Spirit with the flesh, Gal 5 :17; of the fruits of the Spirit, Gal 5:22; of crucifying the flesh, Gal 5:24; Col 3:5; of taking the cross, Matt 16:24; of putting on the new man, Eph 4:24; of thinking on things virtuous, Phil 4:8; and of growing in grace, 1 Pet 2:2. The believer is consecrated to God by the sacrifice of Christ; therefore he must live unto God" (ibid., 185).

53. Hoenecke, *Evangelical Lutheran Dogmatics*, 3:395.

sanctification, is determinative to one's standing before God. There is a pastoral concern here in insuring that Christians do not fall into despair over their lack of sanctification, but continually cling to God's complete act and promise found in justification. Voigt remarks of justification that "the Christian never gets beyond this. His whole life is lived in this relation of forgiveness for Christ's sake."[54] Without neglecting the reality of sanctification, Voigt contends that "there is a beginning, progress and perfecting of the life of faith, but all is in the state of justification and under the grace of the Holy Spirit imparted in it . . . [Justification] is the divine background and substratum of the life of faith."[55] This defends against the idea that justification is merely a past event in the *ordo salutis* that is to be disregarded in the pursuit of sanctified living.[56] Thus it is the centrality of the doctrine of justification, and the avowed rejection of any theology of Christian perfection, that differentiates a Lutheran from an Eastern approach to progress in the life of faith.

The centrality of justification in the Lutheran tradition is seen in the confession that sanctification is "the new spiritual nature [καινός άνθρωπος, πνεῦμα], created through justification."[57] Hoenecke calls sanctification "the fruit of justification and of rebirth."[58] These two redemptive acts are not divorced from one another, but share an intimate connection. Justification causes the birth of a new nature that demonstrates itself through the performance of good works. This renewal of nature occurs through Word and Sacrament, so that where forgiveness is received, God's sanctifying action is also at work. Thus baptism, the Eucharist, and Holy Absolution are all acts which forgive sins, and consequently, grant spiritual life and renewal.

Sanctification can, in one sense, be said to be that which produces good works, but "in another respect good works are identical with sanctification, since sanctification *in concreto* takes place

54. Voigt, *Biblical Dogmatics*, 171.

55. Ibid.

56. See Cooper, "Lutheran Response to Justification."

57. Pieper, *Christian Dogmatics*, 3:5.

58. Hoenecke, *Lutheran Dogmatics*, 3:399.

through the performance of good acts."[59] This is consistent with the Pauline usage in 1 Thess 4:2.[60] These good works are not optional for faith, but necessary. Hoenecke contends that "God demands good works as the necessary fruit of faith and of the fellowship of faith with Christ."[61] Hoenecke goes on to call them "the necessary proof of faith" and "necessary beyond question," arguing that it can even be said that "the Lord grants a reward for sanctification and good works,"[62] although these works are only rewarded insofar as their imperfections are covered by the merits of Christ. Thus, it is necessary not only to perform good works, but for preachers to exhort their people to do so. Pieper encourages pastors to do this, writing: "in urging members of their churches to become 'rich in good works,' pastors should not be deterred from doing this boldly and resolutely, without any fear or faltering, by the thought that this insistence on good works might crowd out of its central position the doctrine of justification without works."[63] This echoes Luther's own words against the antinomians who refused to preach the law. He states:

> They preach only about the redemption of Christ. It is proper to extol Christ in our preaching; but Christ is the Christ and has acquired redemption from sin and death for this very purpose that the Holy Spirit should change our Old Adam into a new man, that we are to be dead unto sin and live unto righteousness, as Paul teaches Rom 6.2 ff., and that we are to begin this change and increase in this new life here and consummate it hereafter.

59. Pieper, *Christian Dogmatics*, 3:5.

60. "For this is the will of God, your sanctification: that you abstain from sexual immorality; that each one of you know how to control his own body in holiness and honor, not in the passion of lust like the Gentiles who do not know God; that no one transgress and wrong his brother in this matter, because the Lord is an avenger in all these things, as we told you beforehand and solemnly warned you. For God has not called us for impurity, but in holiness. Therefore whoever disregards this, disregards not man but God, who gives his Holy Spirit to you" (1 Thess 4:2–8).

61. Hoenecke, *Lutheran Dogmatics*, 3:417.

62. Ibid., 3:425.

63. Pieper, *Christian Dogmatics*, 3:38.

> For Christ has gained for us not only grace (*gratiam*), but also the gift (*donum*), of the Holy Ghost, so that we obtain from Him not only forgiveness of sin, but also the ceasing from sin. Anyone, therefore, who does not cease from his sin, but continues in his former evil way, must have obtained a different Christ, from the Antinomians. The genuine Christ is not with them, even if they cry with the voice of all the angels, Christ! Christ! They will have to go to perdition with their new Christ.[64]

The Lutheran and Eastern Orthodox traditions share a common concern for good works. However, in the Lutheran tradition, these good works are motivated by "the pure grace of God, which we have experienced in Christ Jesus."[65] Good works and sanctification are always to be spoken of with the doctrine of justification in view, so as to avoid moralism and give the proper motivation for producing good deeds.

Sanctification is a process. Because sin clings to the believer throughout life, gaining freedom from sin is a daily struggle. Quenstedt states that "our renovation progresses from day to day, and is to be continued through life, 2 Cor. 4:16."[66] Contrasting sanctification against justification, Gerberding writes: "Justification, being purely an act of God is *instantaneous* and complete; sanctification being a work in which man has a share, is *progressive*."[67] He also argues that God's manner of creation, as demonstrated in the growth of plants and animals, mirrors the way in which God effects salvation in the sinner. As Gerberding exlains, "growth is the law of the kingdom of nature. And the same God operates in the kingdom of Grace, and indeed, much to the same order."[68] In this way, salvation can be spoken of not only as a past event *extra nos*, but also

---

64. Luther, *Concerning Councils and Churches*, quoted in Walther, *Proper Distinction*, 121–22.

65. Pieper, *Christian Dogmatics*, 3:48.

66. Schmid, *Doctrinal Theology*, 506.

67. Gerberding, *Way of Salvation*, 188, emphasis Gerberding's.

68. Ibid., 192–93.

as something that is continually happening inside of us, as God's Spirit is active in killing sin and raising the new Christian to life.

While the believer is being sanctified, he or she is being renewed in God's own image. Hollaz states that "as the body of sin in process of time is more and more weakened by the regenerate man, so the regenerate man is transformed more and more into the image of God from glory to glory by the Holy Spirit."[69] Through the fall, Adam lost the divine image along with the Holy Spirit. This effect of the fall is reversed through Christ, through whom this divine image is restored. As Gerhard states, the "image of God consists in righteousness, true holiness, and the true knowledge of God."[70] These things are restored by the act of "metamorphosis, or transformation" that "is brought about by the Spirit of God, that is, by the one who once created the first man in his own image."[71] This results in "the renewal of the spirit and . . . the putting on of the new man."[72]

There is synergism in sanctification, speaking in the narrow sense of the term. Broadly speaking, salvation is monergistic, including regeneration, justification, and perseverance in the faith. However, there is cooperation between the believer and God in the *process* of sanctification. Quenstedt confesses that "through powers divinely granted man becomes a συνεργόζ of God in his continuing renewal."[73] It is to be remembered, however, that this cooperation is only partial. God's grace is primary, and whatever cooperation the believer has is only due to the new nature that God has granted. Quensdedt argues that the "regenerate man co-operates with God in the work of sanctification, but not by an equal action, but in subordination and dependence on the Holy Spirit, because he does not work with native but with granted powers."[74]

---

69. Schmid, *Doctrinal Theology*, 506.

70. Chemnitz and Gerhard, *Doctrine of Man*, 63.

71. Ibid.

72. Ibid.

73. Hoenecke, *Lutheran Dogmatics*, 3:401.

74. Schmid, *Doctrinal Theology*, 507.

Thus the Lutheran Church confesses synergism in sanctification, while also being careful to confess the primacy of divine grace.

Mystical union and sanctification are intimately related realities. The Christian's good works and holiness are a gift of God, given through divine indwelling. As Calov states, "Sanctification is a work of the Holy Trinity, by which it consecrates us, in body and soul, as its temple, filling us with virtues of every kind, expelling faults of every kind, and conferring upon us the grace of God and the kingdom of heaven."[75] The imagery of a temple is commonly used in discussions of the mystical union. Just as God fills the believer with himself, so also does he fill the believer with good works and grace. Thus, as God's presence increases, indwelling sin and evil decreases.

Conclusion

It has been demonstrated the theosis is not foreign to the Lutheran Confessional tradition. Although the explicit language of deification is not utilized, the concept is readily apparent. For Luther, salvation involves both event (justification), and process (theosis). There are forensic and participatory aspects to God's salvific work. Union with God is initiated by faith, and it is strengthened through the sacramental life of the church. Melanchthon doesn't use explicit participationist language in the Apology, but he does purport that Christians grow daily in holiness, and that justification involves ontological renewal. The Formula explicitly affirms mystical union with God, though it is confessed that mystical union and justification should not be conflated with one another. Finally, it has been demonstrated that the Lutheran Scholastic tradition also teaches a form of deification under the term "mystical union." The dogmaticians argued that God is present in believers not only by way of his gifts, but also by way of his person. This union is Trinitarian insofar as all three persons of the Trinity dwell within believers. However, there is also a specific Christological

75. Ibid., 505.

focus, because this union occurs as a result of Christ's incarnation and the benefits of redemption that are received through Word and Sacrament. The Lutheran tradition also places a consistent emphasis on sanctification, arguing that believers progress in holiness through the indwelling Trinity, and even that they cooperate in this work. It is to be remembered, however, that this work is always imperfect prior to death, and is based upon justification by grace through faith.

3

Theosis in Holy Scripture

THE QUESTION OF THEOSIS in the New Testament is of primary import to the Reformation tradition. Coming from a Lutheran perspective, I adopt the *sola scriptura* principle, and thus judge all theology according to the testimony of Scripture. There are various texts that have been used to support the concept of deification, and a strong case can be made using these texts for an ontological renewal of humankind through union with Christ. This comports with the idea of Christification as expounded upon by the Apostolic Fathers, Irenaeus, Justin Martyr, and Athanasius, as will be demonstrated below. In the New Testament particularly, there is evidence that the Christian participates in a real-ontic union with God through Christ. This union is begun in the sacrament of baptism, and strengthened by the Eucharist. The goal of this union is eschatological transformation, wherein the physical self is changed through union with God.

2 Pet 1:4

His divine power has granted to us all things that pertain to life and godliness, through the knowledge of him who called us to his own glory and excellence, by which he has granted to us his precious and very great promises, so that through them you may become partakers of the divine nature, having escaped from the corruption that is in the world because of sinful desire. (2 Pet 1:3–4)

This verse from 2 Peter is probably the most common text used to argue for the concept of deification.[1] It is the only place in the New Testament where it is bluntly stated that the human Christian partakes in the divine nature. Thus, this text is of primary import to this study, in order that we may examine whether the concept of deification is a biblical idea. However, before getting into the text itself, some preliminary remarks need to be made regarding the canonicity of 2 Peter.

The canon of all three major Christian groups—Roman Catholic, Eastern Orthodox, and Protestant—contain the book of 2 Peter. However, it is notable that 2 Peter is hardly ever cited in the early church, and is not present in all accounts of the New Testament canon. These factors, along with the similarities between Peter and Jude, have caused many scholars to reject Petrine authorship, which would negate the importance of this particular text in support of the biblical notion of theosis.[2] If 2 Peter is not Petrine, the text is of historical value, but cannot establish the veracity of this doctrine. In the Lutheran tradition a distinction, taken from Eusebius,[3] is made between homologoumena and antilogoumena. The homologoumena are undisputed books—those that were not subject to doubt in the early church, such as the thirteen Pauline epistles and the four Gospels. The antilogoumena are disputed books, such as Jude, Hebrews, and 2 Peter. The Lutheran fathers argued that doctrine is to be established on the basis of the undisputed books, rather than the disputed. This is an important caveat to any discussion of this passage. If there were no other indication in the New Testament of theosis, then the doctrine of deification could not be taught on account of this passage alone. There are two reasons why I still think this passage is important to discuss. First,

---

1. See Keating, *Deification and Grace*, 33–37; Russell, *Fellow Workers with God*, 65–69; Starr, "Does 2 Peter 1:4 Speak of Deification?" 81–92; Finlan, "Second Peter's Notion."

2. See for example, Bauckham's discussion in Bauckham, *Jude and 2 Peter*, 137–38.

3. Eusebius, *Church History*, 3.

I adopt Petrine authorship, as uncommon as that position may be.[4] Thus, the teachings of 2 Peter are representative of apostolic teaching. Second, there is evidence for theosis throughout the rest of the New Testament, including the non-disputed Pauline epistles. Thus, this text serves to clarify teaching that is extant in other New Testament literature.

The above text from Peter's second epistle is unfortunately short, and includes only a brief statement of theosis made in passing. What this text does demonstrate is that the doctrine to which Peter is referring was so commonly accepted that he does not have to explicitly define the concept when writing to the church. Interestingly, the early fathers do not often cite this text, and thus it is not used as a basis on which theosis is taught. This further demonstrates that the church's teaching on deification goes beyond the mere words of Peter in this epistle. It is a teaching inherent in the gospel itself, especially as explained by the Apostle Paul.

Some have argued that the text from Peter is an unfortunate imposition of Hellenistic ideas into the early church.[5] This arises from Harnack's approach to the early church, which views the apostolic faith as having been slowly infiltrated by Greek philosophy and ideology, eventually eclipsing the original message of Jesus.[6] It is true that Peter uses Platonic language in this text, but rather than simply adopting Platonism full force, Peter is utilizing common philosophical language and placing it on Christological grounds.[7] Indeed, there are important distinctions between Christian deification and Greek deification. In Greek philosophy, the soul is necessarily immortal by its similarity with the divine nature; in Christian thought, immortality is a gift given to the soul by God,

---

4. See Kruger, "Authenticity of 2 Peter," 645–71; Barker, *New Testament Speaks*, 349–52; Franzmann, *Word of the Lord Grows*, 226–32.

5. Drewery, "Deification," 33–62.

6. Von Harnack, *History of Dogma*, 2:227–30.

7. Finlan finds Middle-Platonic influence in 2 Peter, especially in his utilization of the term *epithymia*, which both Plato and the author of 2 Peter identify with the lowest parts of the human creature as opposed to knowledge, which is the most noble characteristic of man (Finlan, "Second Peter's Notion," 33).

not inherent in nature.[8] In the Greek tradition, deification is attained through knowledge and the control of the passions through philosophical study;[9] in Christianity, theosis is a gift of divine grace, received in Christ. Most importantly, in Greek thought God is not usually identified as personal, whereas in Christianity participation in God is always through contact with a personal, Trinitarian God.[10] Certain terminological and conceptual similarities with the Greek philosophical tradition do not negate the veracity of Peter's doctrine. Like Paul and the author of Hebrews, Peter is willing to utilize philosophical terminology when it can be used to accurately portray the Christian gospel.

The debate in this passage among commentators is over exactly what it means to be a "partaker of the divine nature" (2 Pet 1:4). Luther expounds upon this text with the following words:

> This we have, Peter says, through the power of faith, namely, that we are partakers of and enjoy the fellowship and communion with the divine nature. This is a passage the like of which is not found in the New and Old Testaments; although it is a small matter with unbelievers that we should have fellowship with the very divine nature itself. But what is the nature of God? It is eternal righteousness, wisdom, eternal life, peace, joy, and happiness, and everything good that can be named. Now whoever becomes a partaker of the nature of God receives all this, namely, he lives forever, possesses endless peace, pleasure and joy, and is sincere, pure, just and almighty against Satan, sin and death. Therefore Peter will say: As impossible as it is to separate eternal life and eternal truth from the nature of God, just so impossible is it to separate them from you. Whatever one does to you, he must do to him, for whoever will crush

---

8. Lenz, "Deification of the Philosopher," 50–54.

9. Lenz notes that in Aristotle, "our reason, is the highest and most godlike part of us. Reason is also the most spiritual and celestial, the least bodily part of our souls" (ibid., 55–56).

10. See Daniel Wilson's dissertation on this topic, in which he demonstrates the various differences between the Patristic doctrine of deification and the Hellenistic notions of deification and apotheosis (Wilson, *Deification and the Rule*).

> a Christian must crush God. All this is contained in the
> words, "the divine nature"; and Peter chose these words
> for the purpose to include all in them; and it is truly a
> great thing if one believes it.[11]

Though Luther admits that such strong language of divinization is not present in the rest of Scripture, he is willing to take the text at face value; it talks about real participation in divinity. He refers to this as fellowship and communion. In Luther's view, partaking of divinity in this passage primarily has to do with certain attributes of God that are transferred to the believer through the communion initiated by faith. Thus, Luther purports that the Christian receives divine righteousness, life, immortality, joy, holiness, and peace. This is consistent with Luther's emphasis on the great exchange wherein God gives his righteousness for human sin. In this text, as well as others in Luther's writings, it becomes clear that the great exchange motif includes other divine attributes, rather than simply the righteousness of Christ. This is the context in which theosis is placed in Luther's theology, as is evidenced by his treatment of 2 Peter.

Such an interpretation is not unique to Luther, but is embedded with the tradition of the Reformation. Calvin argues similarly when writing on this passage.[12] He states:

---

11. Luther, *Commentary on Jude and Peter*, 236–37.

12. Mosser writes, "With classic theosis language, Calvin interprets the meaning of the phrase, 'partakers of the divine nature,' in terms of being raised up to God and united with him. He writes: 'We must take into account whence it is that God raises us to such a peak of honour. We know how worthless is the condition of our nature, and the fact that God makes Himself ours so that all His possessions become in a sense ours is a grace the magnitude of which our minds can never fully grasp.' Contemplation of this 'ought to give us abundant cause to renounce the world entirely and be borne aloft to heaven.' Calvin then boldly states: 'We should notice that it is the purpose of the Gospel to make us sooner or later like [conformes] God; indeed it is, so to speak, a kind of deification [quasi deificari].' The older translation conveys the boldness of the thought more adequately: 'Let us then mark, that the end of the gospel is, to render us eventually conformable to God, and, if we may so speak, to deify us.' In concert with the patristic writers Calvin views the believer's partaking of the divine nature as a kind of deification" (Mosser, "Greatest Possible Blessing," 41).

For we must consider from whence it is that God raises us up to such a height of honor. We know how abject is the condition of our nature; that God, then, should make himself ours, so that all his things should in a manner become our things, the greatness of his grace cannot be sufficiently conceived by our minds. Therefore this consideration alone ought to be abundantly sufficient to make us to renounce the world and to carry us aloft to heaven. Let us then mark, that the end of the gospel is, to render us eventually conformable to God, and, if we may so speak, to deify us.[13]

Calvin is willing to utilize the language of deification to an extent when expounding upon this passage, though he is quick to clarify that "the word *nature* is not here essence but *quality.*"[14] Calvin fears the temptation to teach that human nature would become swallowed up in the divine nature, and so it careful to distinguish between God's essence and participation in divine qualities. The apostolic teaching of theosis is that "we shall be partakers of divine and blessed immortality and glory, so as to be, as it were, one with God as far as our capacities will allow."[15] In approaching the essence/energies distinction of Palamas, Calvin purports that humanity participates in God's glory, immortality, and holiness, rather than God's own essence. This preserves the creature/Creator divide that is so central to Calvin's thought.[16]

Luther and Calvin's interpretations of this text are both particularly insightful.[17] For both of these authors, Peter is speaking about an actual participation in divinity. Both Reformers are care-

---

13. Calvin, *Commentaries on the Catholic Epistles,* "2 Peter 1:4."

14. Ibid.

15. Ibid.

16. Calvin is even willing to make a comparison between the Christian and Platonic doctrines of deification: "This doctrine was not altogether unknown to Plato, who everywhere defines the chief good of man to be an entire conformity to God" (ibid.).

17. For further resources on Calvin's view of deification, see Billings, "John Calvin"; Mosser, "Greatest Possible Blessing"; Wedgeworth, "Reforming Deification."

ful not to teach an absorption of the human nature that would destroy the distinction between the creature and Creator, and they do this by placing theosis into the context of the transfer of divine qualities, primarily immortality.

The correctness of this interpretation is demonstrated by the context of the verse in question. Peter describes a number of God's attributes, as well as those given to believers. The section begins by speaking about God's "power," which is used to give "life" as well as "godliness," and "knowledge." God also grants believers escape from corruption and the mortification of sin. Starr defines six qualities in 2 Peter which are transferred to believers: "God and Christ's righteousness or justice . . . 'His' divine power . . . Divine glory . . . Divine excellence or virtue," and centrally incorruptibility and eternality.[18] These are divine qualities that are transferred from the Trinitarian God to his creatures. As Russel explains, "the divine nature (*physis*) in which we are to share through God's gifts is not his essential being but his attributes of glory (*doxa*) and goodness (*arête*)."[19] This is consistent with Luther and Calvin's distinction between God's essential being and the attributes that he shares with believers.

Following the claim that we may participate in the divine nature, Peter gives a number of exhortations to his readers:

> For this very reason, make every effort to supplement your faith with virtue, and virtue with knowledge, and knowledge with self-control, and self-control with steadfastness, and steadfastness with godliness, and godliness with brotherly affection, and brotherly affection with love. For if these qualities are yours and are increasing, they keep you from being ineffective or unfruitful in the knowledge of our Lord Jesus Christ. For whoever lacks these qualities is so nearsighted that he is blind, having forgotten that he was cleansed from his former sins. Therefore, brothers, be all the more diligent to confirm your calling and election, for if you practice these qualities you will never fall. For in this way there

18. Starr, "Does 2 Peter 1:4 Speak of Deification?" 82.

19. Russell, *Fellow Workers with God*, 65.

will be richly provided for you an entrance into the eternal kingdom of our Lord and Savior Jesus Christ. (2 Pet 1:5–11)

These actions and behaviors that are commanded by Peter are given in light of the fact that one is a "partaker of the divine nature." Here he expounds upon the moral aspect of deification. The divine gift of salvation and immortality are grounds by which the Christian can then live a virtuous life, attain godliness, and grow in knowledge.[20]

What is notable about Peter's notion of deification in this text is his Christocentrism. While Peter is certainly willing to engage the language of neoplatonism and possibly Stoicism, his approach to theosis is distinguished from these philosophical traditions by its Christological character. For Peter, there is no "divinization" in the abstract, whereby humans can participate in God through the study of philosophy. Rather, people receive divine qualities through faith in, and knowledge of, Christ. Peter begins his epistle by speaking of the "righteousness of our God and Savior Jesus Christ" (2 Pet 1:1) as well as the "knowledge of God and of Jesus our Lord" (2 Pet 1:2). It is only through the righteousness and knowledge of Christ that we can, in any sense, become partakers of the divine nature. The "power" ($\delta\upsilon\nu\alpha\mu\iota\varsigma$) that Peter identifies as the instrument of our deification is, later in the chapter, identified with the "coming of our Lord Jesus Christ" (2 Pet 1:16). Peter also notes that the final goal of theosis is "entrance into the eternal kingdom of our Lord and Savior Jesus Christ" (2 Pet 1:11). Christ is present in each stage of deification. It is initiated by the divine power manifested in Christ, through which God's own attributes are given to believers. This includes Christ's own righteousness and knowledge. Through the gift of this divine power, the Christian can live in virtue and grow in the knowledge of Christ. Finally, the eschatological goal of union with Christ in his eternal kingdom is received by all who have received such divine blessings. Thus,

---

20. This leads Finlan to conclude, "For Second Peter, divinization means escaping such corruption, and taking on a Godly character" (Finlan, "Second Peter's Notion," 45).

Christification

Peter's theology of divine participation could rightly be called "Christification."

Theosis in the Pauline Corpus: Gorman's Proposal

There have been a number of recent attempts to argue for a doctrine of theosis in Paul's theology. Perhaps the most comprehensive treatment of this subject is that by Michael J. Gorman. For Gorman, the center of Pauline thought is not to be found in forensic justification (Luther), nor is it to be found in the concept of covenant community (N.T. Wright). Rather, "theosis is the center of Paul's theology."[21] Theosis, for Gorman, is a thoroughly Christological reality, and thus is compatible with our proposal of "Christification." While there are similarities between Gorman's idea of theosis and the Eastern Orthodox tradition, they are not synonymous concepts. For Gorman, theosis is primarily cruciformity. God's nature is cruciform, and thus theosis is living the cruciform life, mirroring God's self-giving love. This is demonstrated by the proposal that the *Carmen Christi* of Phil 2:6–11 is Paul's "master story." This text serves as a lens through which Paul's theology is to be read. Gorman argues convincingly that the phrase "although he was in the form of God" can be read "because he was in the form of God."[22] In other words, the incarnation is not contrary to God's normal manner of acting, but is thoroughly consistent with Gods character. In fact, it is the ultimate revelation of God's character. Thus, in contrast to human perceptions of divinity, which are linked with political power, God's power in shown in weakness. It is of God's essence and character to be self-giving.[23] In

21. Gorman, *Inhabiting the Cruciform God*, 170.

22. Ibid., 27.

23. "In this reading, Christ *exercised* his deity. What is *out* of character for normal divinity in our misguided perception of the reality of the form of God is actually *in* character for *this* form of God. That is, although Christ was in the form of God, which leads us to certain expectations, he subverted and deconstructed those expectations when he emptied and humbled himself, which he did *because* he was the *true* form of God" (ibid., emphasis Gorman's).

56

Gorman's words, "divinity has kenotic servanthood as its essential attribute."[24] Theosis then takes this same form; through theosis, the believer is incorporated into Christ and offers him or herself up to others in a cruciform manner.

Gorman also proposes that Paul's doctrine of justification has been misunderstood by the Reformation tradition. For Gorman, justification is not a purely forensic reality, but is thoroughly participatory. Trying to overcome the division common in Pauline studies between juridical and participationist soteriology, Gorman contends that "Paul has not two soteriological models (juridical and participationist) but one, justification by co-crucifixion, meaning restoration to right covenantal relations with God and others by participation in Christ's quintessential covenantal act of faith and love on the cross."[25] Justification is a covenantal category, and it involves participation in Christ's death and resurrection. The believer, through faith, is thus incorporated into Christ and is "co-crucified" with Jesus. Through this crucifixion, covenantal relations are restored. This involves both the restoration of one's relationship with God, and the restoration of the relationship one has with fellow man. For Gorman, Paul's association in Gal 2 between justification and Christ's death demonstrates that "justification by faith, then, is a death-and-resurrection experience."[26] Justification involves incorporation into Christ's death and resurrection through one's own death and resurrection.

Gorman provides conclusive evidence that there is a teaching of theosis in Paul's theology. Consider, for example, the text of Gal 2:

> But if, in our endeavor to be justified in Christ, we too were found to be sinners, is Christ then a servant of sin? Certainly not! For if I rebuild what I tore down, I prove myself to be a transgressor. For through the law I died to the law, so that I might live to God. I have been crucified with Christ. It is no longer I who live, but Christ who lives in me. And the life I now live in the flesh I

24. Ibid., 31.
25. Ibid., 45.
26. Ibid., 69.

> live by faith in the Son of God, who loved me and gave
> himself for me. I do not nullify the grace of God, for if
> righteousness were through the law, then Christ died for
> no purpose. (Gal 2:17–21)

In this text, Paul connects justification in Christ to crucifixion with Christ and divine indwelling. Gorman proposes that "when Paul returns explicitly to the subject of justification in 2:21, he does so having spoken of co-crucifixion with Christ, thereby associating participation in Christ with justification."[27] There is evidence in the context of this chapter that Gorman's argument is essentially correct. In this text, Paul is discussing Christ as the instrument of justification, through faith, rather than the law. The law, which Paul says does not justify, is something that the believer must "die to." The Christian does this by co-crucifixion with Christ and the reception of Christ's person in faith. Paul connects justification here both with the historical event of Christ's death and existential participation in Christ's death and resurrection. Through this act of justification, Christ is given to the believer so that his indwelling establishes the Christian's identity.

The fact that Paul argues against justification by the works of the law with participatory language is quite telling. Paul is not content to speak merely in legal categories, for his argument includes the categories of death and resurrection as well as the indwelling of Christ. This demonstrates that Paul's thoughts on justification are not divorced from his concern for participation in God. However, Gorman is not entirely convincing in eschewing the Reformation's legal approach to justification in Paul. Gorman does not, for example, address Rom 8:

> What then shall we say to these things? If God is for us,
> who can be against us? He who did not spare his own
> Son but gave him up for us all, how will he not also with
> him graciously give us all things? Who shall bring any
> charge against God's elect? It is God who justifies. Who
> is to condemn? Christ Jesus is the one who died—more

27. Ibid., 66.

than that, who was raised—who is at the right hand of God, who indeed is interceding for us. (Rom 8:31–34)

One of the primary arguments against the Roman Catholic understanding of justification since the Reformation has been this text. In this section of Romans, Paul uses legal language that is most apparent in the contrast he draws between condemnation and justification. Because God justifies, no one can condemn. This makes it apparent that in Paul's mind, justification is the opposite of condemnation. It is a legal category, denying that "any charge" can be brought against the elect, because God is "for us." Hodge argues similarly:

> To condemn is to pronounce guilty; or worthy of punishment. To justify is to declare not guilty; or that justice does not demand punishment; or that the person concerned cannot justly be condemned . . . Against the elect in Christ no ground of condemnation can be presented. God pronounces them just, and therefore no one can pronounce them guilty.[28]

Gorman also lacks an extensive discussion of Rom 4, which would seem to contradict his redefinition of justification:

> What then shall we say was gained by Abraham, our forefather according to the flesh? For if Abraham was justified by works, he has something to boast about, but not before God. For what does the Scripture say? "Abraham believed God, and it was counted to him as righteousness." Now to the one who works, his wages are not counted as a gift but as his due. And to the one who does not work but believes in him who justifies the ungodly, his faith is counted as righteousness, just as David also speaks of the blessing of the one to whom God counts righteousness apart from works: "Blessed are those whose lawless deeds are forgiven, and whose sins are covered; blessed is the man against whom the Lord will not count his sin." (Rom 4:1–8)

28. Hodge, *Systematic Theology*, 3:121–22.

Paul connects justification with the imputation of righteousness. He does so in the context of Abraham's believing in contrast to working. If one works and receives a payment, payment is made in accordance with the work done. In justification, one does not work, yet receives righteousness as a gift. The contrast Paul draws is between a righteousness that is "counted" based on works and one that is "counted" based on faith without works. Note also the citation from David that Paul marshals to defend his concept of justification by faith apart from works. The language David uses speaks of forgiveness, covering, and the non-imputation of sin. The logic of Paul's argument is that justification is the imputation of righteousness based on faith, received as a gift rather than as a result of works. This is further expounded upon as the explanation of Ps 32, wherein sin is not imputed. All of this demonstrates that the historic Lutheran approach to justification is exegetically tenable. Justification, for Paul, involves the imputation of righteousness through faith, as well as the non-imputation of sin.[29]

Gorman's proposal that Paul's soteriology is more multifaceted than has often been admitted is correct. There is indeed a connection between justification and resurrection in Paul which involves participation in Christ's death and resurrection. This need not, however, negate a Lutheran reading of Paul. For Paul, justification is a legal term used to identify the status of eschatological vindication placed on the believer. It involves the imputation of righteousness and the non-imputation of sin. Justification also initiates a mystical union between the believer and Christ, wherein the believer participates in Christ's death and resurrection. This union subsequently manifests itself through the believer's self-giving love. Theosis is thus a thoroughly Pauline theme that does not replace forensic justification, but stands alongside it as a complimentary soteriological reality.

---

29. For a defense of this position, see Westerholm, *Perspectives Old and New*, 384–401; Schreiner, "Justification," 19–34; Gathercole, *Where Is Boasting?* 232–48.

Finlan's Proposal for Deification in Paul

Stephen Finlan proposes three Pauline texts that he believes teach theosis. The first text is from 1 Cor 15:

> But someone will ask, "How are the dead raised? With what kind of body do they come?" You foolish person! What you sow does not come to life unless it dies. And what you sow is not the body that is to be, but a bare kernel, perhaps of wheat or of some other grain. But God gives it a body as he has chosen, and to each kind of seed its own body. For not all flesh is the same, but there is one kind for humans, another for animals, another for birds, and another for fish. There are heavenly bodies and earthly bodies, but the glory of the heavenly is of one kind, and the glory of the earthly is of another. There is one glory of the sun, and another glory of the moon, and another glory of the stars; for star differs from star in glory.
>
> So is it with the resurrection of the dead. What is sown is perishable; what is raised is imperishable. It is sown in dishonor; it is raised in glory. It is sown in weakness; it is raised in power. It is sown a natural body; it is raised a spiritual body. If there is a natural body, there is also a spiritual body. Thus it is written, "The first man Adam became a living being"; the last Adam became a life-giving spirit. But it is not the spiritual that is first but the natural, and then the spiritual. The first man was from the earth, a man of dust; the second man is from heaven. As was the man of dust, so also are those who are of the dust, and as is the man of heaven, so also are those who are of heaven. Just as we have borne the image of the man of dust, we shall also bear the image of the man of heaven.
>
> I tell you this, brothers: flesh and blood cannot inherit the kingdom of God, nor does the perishable inherit the imperishable. Behold! I tell you a mystery. We shall not all sleep, but we shall all be changed, in a moment, in the twinkling of an eye, at the last trumpet. For the trumpet will sound, and the dead will be raised imperishable, and we shall be changed. For this perishable body must

> put on the imperishable, and this mortal body must put
> on immortality.

According to Finlan, this text demonstrates that the goal of Christian existence is eschatological union with God through the reception of a spiritual body. Finlan promotes this conclusion in contrast to the popular interpretation by Wright, which privileges continuity over discontinuity in Paul's discussion of the resurrection body.[30] Finlan shows that there are twenty contrasts drawn in this Pauline text between the old and new bodies: a present/future contrast (1 Cor 15:37), earthly/heavenly contrast (1 Cor 15:40, 47–49), mortal/immortal contrast (1 Cor 15:42, 50, 53–54), a contrast between a body of glory and dishonor (1 Cor 15:43), a contrast between a living being and a life-giving spirit (1 Cor 15:45), and a psychic/pneumatic body contrast (1 Cor 15:44, 46). Finlan concludes from these contrasts, "Paul is not just spelling our different animating principles, but entirely different levels and kinds of life force, nativity, and substance."[31] Finlan's exegesis here is thoroughly convincing; Paul's explanation of the resurrection body is placed within a division between that which is physical and earthly and that which is spiritual and glorious. As Finlan shows, Wright's contention that the distinction here is merely one of "animating principles" doesn't take Paul's language at face value. What Finlan demonstrates here is that Paul's theology shows a strong concept of a "spiritual body" as the final eschatological goal, which comports with a teaching of theosis by which the believer shares eschatologically in God's glory. This is consistent with the patristic identification of theosis with the transfer of the divine attributes of immortality and incorruptibility through faith. In this text, Paul explicitly speaks in this manner.

The second text that Finlan expounds upon is Phil 3:8–11, a section of Paul's writings commonly used to argue for a Reformation understanding of justification:

---

30. Finlan, "*Theosis* in Paul?" 69.

31. Ibid.

> For his sake I have suffered the loss of all things and count
> them as rubbish, in order that I may gain Christ and be
> found in him, not having a righteousness of my own that
> comes from the law, but that which comes through faith
> in Christ, the righteousness from God that depends on
> faith—that I may know him and the power of his resur-
> rection, and may share his sufferings, becoming like him
> in his death, that by any means possible I may attain the
> resurrection from the dead.

In this text, Paul is speaking of a righteousness that is given to him by God. This righteousness is one that does not come from "the law," and in fact is not "his own" in any sense. Rather, this righteousness "depends on faith." Such righteousness is a gift "from God." Though the scope of this volume does not allow us to thoroughly demonstrate this point, I believe that this clearly teaches the concept of imputed righteousness.[32] Through faith, the believer receives the righteousness of Christ and is justified. What is particularly noteworthy in this text for our purposes is its participatory language, as Finlan has also pointed out. Commensurate with Gorman's argument, Paul's theology of justification is connected with participatory realities.

For evidence in this text relating to theosis, Finlan points to verse 10, which speaks of sharing in Christ's sufferings (κοινωνιαν των παθηματων αυτου), and thus participating in his death (συμμαρθιζομενος τω θανατω αυτου). The believer participates in this pattern of death and resurrection. The believer does this not purely in imitation of Christ's passion and resurrection, but through a real participation in the actions and person of Christ.[33] This is connected to Paul's contention that the Christian is justified

32. Consider the argument in Vickers, *Jesus' Blood and Righteousness*, 192–216. Vickers argues here that the concept of the imputation of Christ's active and passive obedience is a thoroughly Pauline concept. He does this by demonstrating that rather than prooftexting, as if one verse specifically teaches this concept, it can be derived by reading the Pauline discussions of justification "synoptically." For Vickers, the themes of justification by faith, imputed righteousness, and the Christological nature of righteousness can be synthesized in Paul's thought to formulate a bold doctrine of imputation.

33. Finlan, "*Theosis* in Paul?" 72–73.

"in him." Thus, it is through union with Christ that the believer is justified (imputed as righteous), and consequently shares in Christ's own death and resurrection. As Gorman demonstrated in Galatians 2, Paul's theology once again connects imputative justification with a death and resurrection experience that occurs as the Christian becomes united with Christ's person.

The participatory theme here does not end with the notion of resurrection, but with eschatological consummation. Paul speaks of the transformation of "our lowly bodies to be like his glorious body, by the power that enables him even to subject all things to himself" (Phil 3:21). Just as the realities of death and resurrection are participatory, so too is the final glorification of the believer. The same power that asserts Christ's divine authority will grant life to the bodies of Christians. In other words, participation in the divine power at work in Christ is the instrument of glorification. This is consistent with Paul's theology of resurrection in 1 Cor 15. Christ's earthly body was put death and a spiritual body was raised; thus, through participation in Christ, the Christian's psychic body dies and is raised in the Spirit, acquiring a pneumatic existence. Finlan notes that "first there is an earthly conformation to the Christlike pattern of dying to sin; then there is reception of godly righteousness and light; and finally there is physical death and resurrection, which entails receiving a transformed body modeled on Christ's body."[34] As in 1 Cor 15, "This is no mere metaphor, but a straightforward attempt to describe the resurrected body the believer will receive."[35] Likewise, Phil 3 demonstrates that participationist language is central to Paul's soteriology and is prominent throughout the process of salvation. In justification, the believer participates in Christ's death and resurrection; in glorification, the Christian participates in Christ's divine power and receives a pneumatic body through his exalted human nature.

The final text that Finlan expounds is from 2 Cor 3:18, which Finlan refers to as the "most frank theotic passage in Paul."[36] The

34. Ibid., 73.
35. Ibid.
36. Ibid., 75.

text states, "And we all, with unveiled face, beholding the glory of the Lord, are being transformed into the same image from one degree of glory to another. For this comes from the Lord who is the Spirit" (2 Cor 3:18). Here, Paul is making reference here to the veil placed over Moses' face so that the Israelites were unable to see the glory of the Lord shown there. In Paul's argument, these veils are lifted for those who believe in Christ. Faith, then, lifts the veil such that Christians become able to see the glory of God and participate in it. Just as Moses' face participated in God's glory, Christians can likewise participate in and reflect his glory. So it is that the Spirit is the active person here, as he gradually increases the believer's participation in God. Finlan writes that "Christ *transmits* God's light to believers, who shine with Christ's glory."[37] This glory is then gradually given to believers "from one degree of glory to another." The goal is eschatological glorification wherein the pneumatic bodies of believers reflect God's own character in light of the incarnate and risen Christ. The plain reading of this text demonstrates that God's glory is something that can be participated in, and also that this participation involves a process of conformity to God's own image.

The three texts that Finlan points to are all indications of a concept of deification in Pauline theology. In 1 Cor 15, Paul argues that Christians await a pneumatic existence through participation in Christ's person. According to Phil 3, this eschatological goal of theosis begins in justification, whereby the believer, along with the imputation of righteousness, experiences a death and resurrection through participation in Christ's suffering and resurrection. Such participation in divine glory transforms the believer until the reception of a pneumatic body at the eschaton. This demonstrates that there are three temporal aspects to Pauline deification: the believer is *presently* deified, having been united to Christ's death and resurrection; the Christian is *being* deified as God's glory transforms human nature; and finally, the Christian *will be* deified at the parousia.

37. Ibid.

Christistification

Union with Christ in Pauline Theology

In his influential book, *The Mysticism of Paul the Apostle*, Albert Schweitzer argues that justification is a "subsidiary crater" in Paul's thinking.[38] For Schweitzer, the center of Paul's thought is not forensic justification, as in Luther, but lies in his Christ-mysticism. Paul's mystical conception is not primarily ethical, but refers instead to the identification of the believer with Christ and the church.[39] Schweitzer purports that the fundamental element of Pauline mysticism is: "I am in Christ; in Him I know myself as a being who is raised above this sensuous, sinful, and transient world and already belongs to the transcendent; in Him I am assured of resurrection; in Him I am a Child of God."[40] This mysticism is commensurate with Schweitzer's interpretation of Jesus as an apocalyptic prophet.[41] Schweitzer's Paul is heavily influenced by Jewish apocalypticism, and thus places this Christ-mysticism within the context of the age to come.[42] Thus, through participation in Christ, specifically in his resurrection, the believer participates in the general resurrection spiritually in the present age.

Though there is not sufficient reason to disregard justification as a tertiary and primarily polemical doctrine in Paul's thought, Schweitzer rightly demonstrates that there is a strong mystical element to Pauline theology. E. P. Sanders further develops this view, arguing that for Paul, transgression is not wrong because it is a

38. Schweitzer, *Mysticism of Paul*, 225.

39. "Paul preaches Christ-Mysticism on the ground of the eschatological concept of the predestined solidarity of the Elect with one another and with the Messiah, as Jesus had done before him, but with the difference, that Paul presents it in the form which it assumes as a consequence of the death and resurrection of Jesus" (ibid., 113).

40. Ibid., 3.

41. See ibid., *Quest of the Historical Jesus*, 330–403.

42. Schweitzer argues that Paul's theology is Jewish rather than Hellenistic: "Whatever views and conceptions are brought up for comparison, the result is always the same—that Paulinism and Greek thought have nothing, absolutely nothing, in common" (ibid., *Mysticism of Paul*, 99).

breach of divine law, but because it severs the believer's mystical union with Christ. As Sanders explains:

> The heart of Paul's thought is not that one ratifies and agrees to a covenantal relation with God and remaining in it on the condition of proper behavior; but that one dies with Christ, obtaining new life and the initial transformation which leads to the resurrection and ultimate transformation, that one is a member of the body of Christ and one Spirit with him, and that one remains so unless one breaks the participatory union by forming another.[43]

Sanders draws on a text from 1 Corinthians to demonstrate this point:

> And God raised the Lord and will also raise us up by his power. Do you not know that your bodies are members of Christ? Shall I then take the members of Christ and make them members of a prostitute? Never! Or do you not know that he who is joined to a prostitute becomes one body with her? For, as it is written, "The two will become one flesh." But he who is joined to the Lord becomes one spirit with him. (1 Cor 6:14–17)

With this text, Paul argues against sexual immorality. Notably, he does not state that such immorality is against the law of God, though Paul surely accepted this as fact, but points instead to the nature of the believer's mystical union with Christ. The one who has been baptized into Christ "is joined to the Lord" and can even be said to become "one spirit with him." This real-ontic union is the basis upon which Paul condemns inappropriate sexual union. The believer cannot become "one flesh" with a prostitute, because the Christian is "one flesh" with Christ. This text validates the Medieval theme of the marriage of the soul with God that informed Luther's mysticism as a genuinely Pauline concept.

Paul's in-Christ mysticism is apparent in many sacramental texts throughout his corpus. Commensurate with the argument against sexual immorality, Paul argues against idolatry with divine

---

43. Sanders, *Paul and Palestinian Judaism*, 514.

union in mind. Paul purports that for Christians to be idolaters is to "be participants with demons" (1 Cor 10:20). Through pagan sacrifice, unbelievers participate in demonic fellowship under the name of false gods. Paul answers this false form of participation with the Eucharistic meal through which Christians experience "participation in the blood of Christ" and "participation in the body of Christ" (1 Cor 10:16). Participation with evil is answered by promoting Eucharistic participation in Christ. Holy Communion, in Paul's thought, is not a purely symbolic or memorial meal, but an event wherein Christians are mystically united with one another and their Lord through his presence in the Eucharistic elements.

Paul's theology of baptism is similarly mystical. He argues that "all of us who have been baptized into Christ Jesus were baptized into his death" (Rom 6:3). Through the act of baptism, the Christian is placed into Christ and experiences a death and resurrection through Christ's own death and resurrection. Paul exhorts the Romans by stating that "we were therefore buried with him by baptism into death" (Rom 6:4). This death is a death to sin, which also results in a resurrection such that "just as Christ Jesus was raised from the dead by the glory of the Father, we too might walk in newness of life" (Rom 6:4). Paul echoes this same thought in Colossians, saying, "having been buried with him in baptism, in which you were also raised with him through faith in the powerful working of God, who raised him from the dead" (Col 2:12). The motivation for holy living, then, is the reality of death and resurrection that occurred objectively at the moment of baptism. As Coniaris rightly states, "Baptism is our own personal Easter. When we are plunged under the waters of baptism, we are not only washed, we *die* to sin. The old sinful nature is drowned. When we rise from the waters, we *rise* to new life in Christ. We share in Christ's death and resurrection."[44] So it is that along with being united to Christ's death and resurrection, believers also "have put on Christ" (Gal 3:27) by baptism. In this way, it becomes apparent that mystical union informs Paul's theology of baptism.

---

44. Coniaris, *Introducing the Orthodox Church*, 130, emphasis Coniaris'.

The notion of union with Christ is an extensive one in Paul's theology. This is made clear in his rejection of false forms of participation, such as sexual immorality and idolatry. Indeed, the union between Christ and the believer is so strong that the two become "one flesh" and "one spirit." This union begins with baptism, wherein the believer is incorporated into Christ, participating in Christ's own death and resurrection through a death to sin and rebirth to righteousness. This union is strengthened by partaking of the Eucharist, wherein the Christian participates in Christ's body and blood. This comports with the Lutheran contention of "mystical union" and establishes a clear teaching of theosis in Paul's theology that centers around Christ's redemptive work as received through Word and Sacrament.

Deification in John's Gospel

John's gospel is known for its especially high Christology, which is supposedly lacking in the Synoptics. It is certainly true that John emphasizes the deity of Christ, and what is significant for our purposes is that Christ's deity is connected to the status of the Christian believer in Johannine theology. The prologue of the fourth Gospel expounds upon Jesus' role in creation, as well as on his unity with the Father in his preexistent state. Christ's incarnation is connected here with the reception of believers into the family of God: "But to all who did receive him, who believed in his name, he gave the right to become children of God, who were born, not of blood nor of the will of the flesh nor of the will of man, but of God" (John 1:12–13). This clearly demonstrates a connection between Christ's incarnation and the believer's union with God. In other words, God became man, so that man might become a child of God.

It is significant that John emphasizes the Trinitarian nature of salvation throughout his gospel. For example, he writes:

> For he whom God has sent utters the words of God, for he gives the Spirit without measure. The Father loves the Son and has given all things into his hand. Whoever

believes in the Son has eternal life; whoever does not obey the Son shall not see life, but the wrath of God remains on him. (John 3:34)

The Trinitarian nature of God is expressed through the language sourrounding the Father's love for the Son and the Father's giving of the Spirit to the Son. This Trinitarian pattern is connected with the salvation of believers. Through faith, the believer receives eternal life; the love of God the Father and the gift of the Spirit are given to the true Christian. Thus, that which Christ has by nature, the believer has by grace.[45]

Discussions on theosis in John's gospel often center on John 10, wherein Jesus calls human beings "gods." John writes: "Jesus answered them, 'Is it not written in your Law, "I said, you are gods"? If he called them gods to whom the word of God came—and Scripture cannot be broken" (John 10:34–35). This text utilizes a quotation from Ps 82 that identifies humans with *elohim*.[46] Finlan proposes that the term *elohim* in Ps 82 is "a label for people who receive the divine quality of deathlessness."[47] Jesus, however, goes beyond an attribution of the title of "gods," used merely to denote immortality, because "he is making a *divinity* connection."[48] The argument Finlan makes is that Jesus is defending his divine status by arguing from the lesser to the greater.

---

45. "So Jesus said to them, 'Truly, truly, I say to you, the Son can do nothing of his own accord, but only what he sees the Father doing. For whatever the Father does, that the Son does likewise. For the Father loves the Son and shows him all that he himself is doing. And greater works than these will he show him, so that you may marvel. For as the Father raises the dead and gives them life, so also the Son gives life to whom he will. The Father judges no one, but has given all judgment to the Son, that all may honor the Son, just as they honor the Father. Whoever does not honor the Son does not honor the Father who sent him. Truly, truly, I say to you, whoever hears my word and believes him who sent me has eternal life. He does not come into judgment, but has passed from death to life," (John 5:19–24).

46. I reject Finlan's contention that "the *elohim* were an 'assembly of gods' over whom Yahweh ruled" (Finlan, "Deification in Jesus' Teaching," 31).

47. Ibid., 32.

48. Ibid.

In this text, Jesus' claims to divinity are called "blasphemy" by the Pharisees, resulting in a desire to stone him: "It is not for a good work that we are going to stone you but for blasphemy, because you, being a man, make yourself God" (John 10:33). In response, Jesus retorts:

> Is it not written in your Law, "I said, you are gods"? If he called them gods to whom the word of God came— and Scripture cannot be broken— do you say of him whom the Father consecrated and sent into the world, "You are blaspheming'" because I said, "I am the Son of God"? If I am not doing the works of my Father, then do not believe me; but if I do them, even though you do not believe me, believe the works, that you may know and understand that the Father is in me and I am in the Father. (John 10:34–38)

Jesus makes the point that divine titles are applied to humans in the Old Testament. If it was not sinful for Old Testament saints to be described as divine, surely it is not blasphemy to declare divinity. Just as there was something divine about certain people in the Old Testament, there is something divine about his own person. Yet Jesus' own person is divine in a unique sense, for he claims, "I and the Father are one" (John 10:30)—a claim which no Old Testament saint would be willing to make. As Jesus makes apparent, those in the old covenant were called gods due to their reception of the divine Word: "he called them gods to whom the word of God came" (John 10:35). In contrast to this, Jesus is called God not as one who receives, but as one who is sent. He describes himself as one whom "the Father consecrated and sent into the world" (John 10:36). Because John opens his gospel by describing Jesus as "the Word," he is likely paralleling those who received the Word old covenant as well as Jesus, who is identified *as* the divine Word. Thus Finlan is correct is contending that Jesus is arguing from the lesser to the greater. If the Old Testament saints were "gods" by virtue of their reception of the word, how much more is Jesus divine, since he is identified *as* the Word? It is clear in this text that Jesus is connecting that which is divine about himself to a similar quality of those in the old covenant who were called "gods." Thus, a concept of deification is inescapable in this text. Because John consistently emphasizes both the Sonship of Christ and the adoption of believers, it is likely that the concepts are interrelated. Adoption implies theosis of some sort, reception of certain divine attributes such as immortality, and fellowship with God's Trinitarian life.

Conclusion

It is apparent that there is a teaching of deification in the New Testament. First Peter explicitly states that believers partake of the divine nature. In line with Luther and Calvin's exegesis of this text, the most preferable reading identifies this partaking of divinity with the transfer of certain divine attributes such as power, glory, incorruptibility, and immortality. Pauline theology also contains an inherent concept of deification. Paul's concept of theosis is thoroughly Christological, and it is based on a participation in Christ's own death and resurrection. There is also a sense of the transferance of divine glory to the believer throughout life, and especially at the resurrection. This is connected to the sacraments of baptism and the Eucharist. Finally, Johannine theology also contains a teaching of deification. In John's gospel, believers can be identified as "gods" through their reception of the divine Word, which is identified with Christ. Jesus' own Sonship grants the status of "sons" to those who receive Christ in faith. It is especially noteworthy that all three of these biblical writers place deification within a Christological context. For Peter, it is the reception of Christ's attributes through participation in God; for Paul, theosis is primarily participation in Christ's own death and resurrection; for John, deification is the reception of the Word, which grants adoption and immortality. This is commensurate with our thesis that deification is best understood as Christification.

4

Theosis as Christification in Early
Patristic Sources

THERE IS A DISTINCTION between the earliest patristic writings and later Eastern theologians who follow Dionysius the Areopogite on the doctrine of theosis. In the Apostolic Fathers and apologists (along with several later fathers), theosis is viewed primarily through the lens of the incarnation, and is, in that sense, Christification. This is principally seen as the transfer of divine qualities such as incorruptibility and immortality that occurs through union with God in conjunction with Christ's incarnation. The focus is soteriological, or as Kharlamov expresses it, "economic." Humankind's union with God is an essential aspect of the divine economy brought about through the Christ-event. Alhough such a teaching comes with ontological implications, philosophical discussions about the union between dissimilar ontological beings have been largely absent in the Apostolic Fathers and apologists. These writers do not make the later distinction between God's essence and energies, nor do they discuss the experiential aspects of deification through contemplative prayer. In this chapter, an examination of Ignatius, Justin Martyr, Irenaeus, and Athanasius will demonstrate the prominence of this Christological approach to theosis.

The Apostolic Fathers

The theme of deification, though not as pronounced as it is in later centuries, is present in the earliest writers in the church. Since the scope of the present work does not permit an examination of all the earliest Christian literature, we will look at Ignatius of Antioch, who offers the most developed and consistent concept of theosis. In his seven epistles, Ignatius emphasizes imitation of God, but does not place theosis purely in this context. While Kharlamov's contention that "in the period of the Apostolic Fathers, imitation of Christ and deification are expressed more in terms of 'economy' than of ontology"[1] is essentially correct, there is an ontological element in Ignatius' concept of theosis that centers on union with Christ.

Ignatius proposes that the Christian is predestined for "unchangeable glory forever,"[2] which occurs through "genuine suffering by the will of the Father and of Jesus Christ our God."[3] The Christian thus imitates the pattern of Christ. The believer suffers in this age, participating in the sufferings of Christ, and consequently participates in Christ's eternal glory.[4] Ignatius implores the Romans, "Allow me to be an imitator of the suffering of my God."[5] In a more extreme statement, Ignatius writes that Jesus' "life is not in us unless we voluntarily choose to die into his suffering."[6] This fits the cruciform picture of theosis painted in Gorman's portrait of Paul, wherein theosis involves participation in Christ's suffering. Such participation in glory is not a purely heavenly reality, but Ignatius can state that Jesus Christ "*has* glorified you."[7] This is all a result of Christ, who is "our inseparable life."[8] Christ, being "the mind of the Father,"[9] brings us into union with God the

---

1. Kharlamov, "Emergence of the Deification Theme," 53.

2. Ign. *Eph.*, 1:1.

3. Ibid., 1:1.

4. This pattern of suffering to glory is prominent in Ignatius' Christology: "There is only one physician, who is both flesh and spirit, born and unborn, God in man, true life in death, both from Mary and from God, first subject to suffering and then beyond it, Jesus Christ our Lord" (ibid., 7:2).

5. Ign. *Rom.*, 6:3.

6. Ign. *Magn.*, 5:2.

7. Ign. *Eph.* 2:2., emphasis mine.

8. Ibid., 3:2.

9. Ibid.

Father, initiating our participation in the Trinitarian life. This participation comes through the church, specifically in its ecclesiastical structure, since the bishops "are in the mind of Christ."[10] Christians should thus be in obedience to their bishop, as Christ is obedient to his Father.[11] Ignatius even calls God the Father "the bishop of all."[12] He urges the Magnesians, "Be subject to the bishop and to one another, as Jesus Christ in the flesh was to the Father, and as the apostles were to Christ and to the Father, that there may be unity, both physical and spiritual."[13]

This reveals that the two most prominent themes in Ignatius' epistles—episcopacy and martyrdom—are placed within the broader context of mystical union. For Ignatius, obedience to the bishop is important due to the mystical nature of the church. Through the institutional church, the believer participates in God through corporate worship.[14] Apart from union with the church's appointed structure through obedience to the episcopal office, Christians risk being cut off from such divine participation. Commensurate with this approach, Ignatius proposes that martyrdom is a blessing because, through death, the believer participates in Christ's own suffering. He urges his readers not to defend his life but to allow him to face death under the emperor; this is not a purely moral concern for Ignatius, as if martyrdom were simply a virtuous act, but is instead rooted in his desire for participation in Christ's sufferings.

---

10. Ibid.

11. "Let us therefore be careful not to oppose the bishop, in order that we may be obedient to God" (ibid., 5:3).

12. Ign. *Magn.*, 3:1.

13. Ibid., 13:2.

14. Quasten writes that "He does not recognize individual independence in the spiritual life or in the mystical union with Christ but acknowledges only one divine union with the Savior, namely that accomplished through liturgical worship. His mysticism springs from the divine cult, which means that it does not center around the individual soul but around the community of the faithful functioning liturgical body" (Quasten, *Patrology*, 1:73).

Ignatius further states that those in the church are "members of his [God's] Son."[15] Through the church's unity, believers "may always have a share in God."[16] This and other statements make it apparent that there is an ontological strand in Ignatius' concept of deification. Christians are "God-bearers and temple-bearers, Christ-bearers, bearers of holy things, adorned in every respect with the commandments of Jesus Christ."[17] Thus, Christian participate in God, bearing God in their own body. Similarly, Ignatius writes that believers "abide in Christ Jesus both physically and spiritually,"[18] negating a purely moral understanding of union with God. He also explicitly states that God "dwells in us, in order that we may be his temples, and he may be in us as our God."[19] Thus, those who believe "bear the stamp of God the Father through Jesus Christ,"[20] as opposed to unbelievers, who "bear the stamp of this world."[21] It is apparent that while martyrdom is a unique event—wherein participation in Christ is uniquely experienced—there are other means of theosis. The structure of Christian life is inherently participatory. Through baptism, all Christians bear God within themselves (as the temple language indicates), and obey the commandments of Christ through this indwelling. This divine life grows throughout the Christian's existence, and comes to its consummation at the moment of glorification.

Ignatius' thought places an emphasis on the *imitatio Christi*, but not a purely as a moralistic concept. Instead, imitation of God comes through one's "new life through the blood of God,"[22] which makes obedience "natural to you."[23] Thus, the life of obedience is rooted in the ontological change that occurs within the Christian

15. Ign. *Eph.*, 4:2.
16. Ibid.
17. Ibid., 9:2.
18. Ibid., 10:3.
19. Ibid., 15:3.
20. Ign. *Magn.*, 5:2.
21. Ibid.
22. Ign. *Eph.*, 1:1.
23. Ibid.

through the blood of Christ. Ignatius also eschews pure perfection-ism by confessing, "I have not yet been perfected in Jesus Christ. For now I am only beginning to be a disciple."[24] He places good works in the context of the new creation, writing: "Those who belong to the flesh cannot do spiritual things, nor can those who are spiritual do fleshly things, just as faith cannot do the things of unfaithfulness, nor unfaithfulness the things of faith."[25] So it is that the deciding factor is not works *per se*, but the state of faith, which determines the manner of works.[26] Ignatius confesses that "even those things that you do according to the flesh are in fact spiritual, for you do everything in Jesus Christ."[27] Ignatius is not moralistic, but argues that good works are grounded in the concrete events of Christ's life, death, and resurrection as received through mystical union that occurs by faith.

There is also a strong sacramental strand of teaching in Igna-tius' concept of theosis. He calls the Eucharist "the medicine of im-mortality, the antidote we take in order not to die but to live forever in Jesus Christ."[28] The Eucharist is not a symbol, but "is the flesh of our savior Jesus Christ, which suffered for our sins and which the Father by his goodness raised up."[29] This occurs through the incarnation of Jesus Christ, which brought "the newness of eternal life"[30] and the "abolition of death."[31] Christ's death also plays an integral role in our salvation. Ignatius proclaims that the cross is "salvation and eternal life to us"[32] and that Jesus "died for us in

---

24. Ibid., 3:1.

25. Ibid., 8:2.

26. "The tree is known by its fruit; thus those who profess to be Christ's will be recognized by their actions. For the work is a matter not of what one promises now, but of persevering to the end in the power of faith" (ibid., 14:2).

27. Ibid., 8:2.

28. Ibid., 20:2.

29. Ign. *Smyrn.*, 6:2.

30. Ign. *Eph.*, 19:3.

31. Ibid., 19:3.

32. Ibid., 18:1.

order that by believing in his death you might escape death."[33] The benefits of this death are given through the waters of holy baptism.[34] The themes of Christ *for us* and Christ *in us* coincide with one another in Ignatius' thought. He consistently appeals to the historical events of Christ's incarnation, death, and resurrection as foundational soteriological realities; however, Ignatius' emphasis on the objective historical action of Jesus does not overshadow the importance of the personal reception of these gifts through the sacramental life of the church.

Ignatius teaches a clear doctrine of deification in a Christological and biblically-based manner. He avoids the philosophical issues that arise in later Eastern theology and is concerned primarily with the salvation of the church. He does not spend time discussing the deification of creation, but focuses on the union that the Christian enjoys with God in light of the incarnation, death, and resurrection of Christ. In Ignatius' theology, Christians are bearers of God because, through faith and baptism, Christians receive divine glory and enjoy the presence of the Holy Trinity. So it is that Christians are remade as new creations and produce good works as a result of the deifying work that God is doing within them. This theotic movement becomes an ecclesiological reality as Christ incorporates himself into his people through baptism and grants the gift of immortality through his flesh in the Eucharist.

The Apologists

Though more philosophical in nature, certain important themes of early Christian theology can be gathered by reading the second-century apologists. Justin Martyr is the most influential and prolific apologist of this era, and thus his writings play a significant role in determining the teaching of theosis in the second- and third-century church. Justin's theology is Christocentric. Justin

---

33. Ign. *Trall.*, 2:1.

34. "He was born and was baptized in order that by his suffering he might cleanse the water" (Ign. *Eph.*, 18:2).

views Christ as a divine figure,[35] most often referred to as the Λογοζ, who became human and, through his incarnation, death, and resurrection, restores humanity to fellowship with God. It is in this Christological context that certain ideas connected with deification appear in Justin's writing. In a statement that aptly summarizes his soteriology, Justin writes:

> He in the beginning did of His goodness, for man's sake, create all things out of unformed matter; and if men by their works show themselves worthy of His design, they are deemed worthy, and so we have received—of reigning in company with Him, being delivered from corruption and suffering. For as in the beginning He created us when we were not, so do we consider that, in like manner, those who choose what is pleasing to Him are, on account of their choice, deemed worthy of incorruption and fellowship with Him.[36]

Through sin, humanity fell into suffering, death, and corruption. Salvation is primarily—for Justin—deliverance from corruption and the reception of divine immortality. Deification is predominantly the reception of divine incorruption, immortality, and a restored fellowship with God.[37] The cross is also a central soteriological reality for Justin.[38] He writes that Christ "became man for our sakes, that, by becoming a partaker of our sufferings,

35. "Both Him, and the Son . . . and the prophetic Spirit, we worship and adore, knowing them in reason and truth, and declaring without grudging to every one who wished to learn, as we have been taught" (*1 Apol.* 6, *ANF* 1:164).

36. Ibid. 10, *ANF* 1:165.

37. As Kharlamov notes, "For him, as for the Apostolic Fathers, the notion of deification is similar to the achievement of immortality, incorruption, and eternal life in the presence of God" (Kharlamov, "Deification in the Apologists," 69).

38. Barnard argues that Justin's philosophically oriented theology has no place for the soteriological significance of the cross, yet Justin inconsistently emphasizes its importance: "The significance of Justin's statements about the Cross should not be underestimated. In strict logic his philosophical presuppositions, which controlled his intellectual apprehension of Christianity, had no place for any objective theory of Atonement" (Barnard, *Justin Martyr*, 125).

He might also being us healing."[39] Christ takes on our nature, that he might heal us by his divine nature. Justin states that "through faith in Him [God]"[40] Christians receive "incorruption."[41] This gift comes through Jesus Christ, who is "[o]ur teacher of these things."[42] Like Ignatius, Justin connects the reception of divine gifts to the sacraments. He writes that through the Eucharist, "our blood and flesh by transmutation are nourished."[43] This transformation of humanity occurs through partaking in the Eucharistic elements. Justin is also the first writer to speak explicitly of people becoming "gods," explaining,

> But as my discourse is not intended to touch on this point, but to prove to you that the Holy Ghost reproaches men because they were made like God, free from suffering and death, provided that they keep His commandments, and were deemed deserving of the name of His sons, and yet they, becoming like Adam and Eve, work out death for themselves; let the interpretation of the Psalm be just as you wish, yet thereby it is demonstrated that all men are worthy of becoming "gods," and of having power to become sons of the Highest; and shall be each by himself judged and condemned like Adam and Eve.[44]

This passage attests to Justin's belief in universal sinfulness and his conviction that death was brought into the world as a result of the fall. There is a free decision whereby humans can either accept and live in death, or escape death through the Christian faith. Justin concludes, based on Ps 81:6, that humans have the capability, through faith, of becoming gods. This concept is closely tied to the reception of immortality and adoption as "sons of the Highest." According to Justin, Christians can become gods through the reception of immortality and adoption as sons.

39. *2 Apol.* 13, *ANF* 1:193.
40. *1 Apol.* 13, *ANF* 1:166.
41. Ibid.
42. Ibid.
43. Ibid. 66, *ANF* 1:185.
44. *Dial.* 124, *ANF* 1:262.

There is a final passage of Justin, taken from a citation in Leonitus of Byzantium's work, *Against Nestorians and Eutychians*, that gives a comprehensive explanation of the fall—which results in the loss of immortality—and the redemption that restores human nature. Justin writes:

> When God formed man at the beginning, He suspended the things of nature on his will, and made an experiment by means of one commandment. For He ordained that, if he kept this he should partake of immortal existence; but if he transgressed it, the contrary should be his lot. Man having been thus made, and immediately looking towards transgression, naturally became subject to corruption. Corruption then becoming inherent in nature, it was necessary that He who wished to save should be one who destroyed the efficient cause of corruption. And this could not otherwise be done than by the life which is according to nature being united to that which has received the corruption, and so destroying the corruption, while preserving as immortal for the future that which had received it. It was therefore necessary that the Word should become possessed of a body, that He might deliver us from the death of natural corruption.[45]

Justin ties the fall to a corruption of nature. The human creature was made like God in the prelapsarian state, with the divine attributes of immortality and incorruptibility. Through the fall, these divine characteristics were lost. Thus, the incarnation is the restoration of mankind's union with God, which involves the reception of divine qualities. There are several important points that can be drawn from this. First, theosis, according to Justin, primarily denotes the reception of divine immortality and incorruption. Second, Justin's view of deification is Christological, being rooted in the incarnation of Christ.

Justin's student, Tatian, writes on similar themes. Speaking of the original creation of the human race, Tatian writes:

45. *Lost Fragments* 11, ANF 1:301.

> For the heavenly Logos, a spirit emanating from the Father and a Logos from the Logos-power, in imitation of the Father who begat Him made man an image of immortality, so that, as incorruption is with God, in like manner, man, sharing in a part of God might have the immortal principle also.[46]

Participation in divinity is inherent in humanity as it was created. In having the *imago dei*, humankind was given the divine attribute of immortality as well as the free will to reject it. Through free decision, humankind lost immortality and fell into sin: "Our free-will has destroyed us; we who were free have become slaves; we have been sold through sin."[47] Redemption involves the restoration of humanity to its intended goal through union with God. Tatian purports that "it becomes us not to seek for what we once had, but have lost, to unite the soul with the Holy Spirit, and to strive after union with God."[48] It is the true essence of humanity to participate in divine attributes rather than mortality.[49] Tatian, like his teacher Justin, expounds upon a doctrine of theosis that is grounded primarily in participation in divine immortality and incorruption through union with God.

Theophilus teaches a similar form of deification, wherein the Christian is said to become "god" by participation in divine immortality. According to Theophilus, humankind was created with the capacity for both immortality and sin, having the free choice to obtain life or death. Theophilus writes:

> Neither, then, immortal nor yet mortal did He make him, but, as we have said above, capable of both; so that if he should incline to the things of immortality, keeping the commandment of God, he should receive as a reward from Him immortality, and should become God; but if,

46. *Address of Tatian to the Greeks* 7, ANF 2:67.

47. Ibid. 11, ANF 2:70.

48. Ibid. 15, ANF 2:71.

49. "But man alone is the image and likeness of God; and I mean by man, not one who performs actions similar to those of animals, but one who has advanced far beyond humanity—to God Himself" (ibid., ANF 2:71).

on the other hand, he should turn to the things of death, disobeying God, he should himself be the cause of death to himself.[50]

The fall caused humankind to forfeit the human destiny of becoming god in falling captive to sin. Salvation involves both the forgiveness of sins and the renewal of the *imago dei*, which together result in participation in God and immortality. Forgiveness of sins is granted "through the water and laver of regeneration."[51] Deification begins when God opens "the eyes of the soul and the ears of the heart"[52] This process is completed at the resurrection, when "thou shalt have put off the mortal, and put on incorruption."[53] The focus, again, is on immortality and incorruption: "and then, having become immortal, thou shalt see the Immortal, if now you believe on Him."[54] Immortality is not, for Theophilus, simply unending life, but there is something transformative about the reception of immortality that makes the believer like God. Kharlamov contends that, in Theophilus, "we have a concept of deification as full human maturity."[55] Kharlamov's statement accurately summarizes the evidence. Deification is the original goal of humanity, though the fall caused humanity to lose the gift of theosis. This original state of humankind is restored through the Christian faith, and those who believe will receive immortality and union with God at the resurrection, thereby achieving God's intended goal for the human race.

In all three of the early apologists examined, deification is a primary soteriological theme. Each emphasizes the free will with which humankind was endowed at creation. Humanity was created for participation in God, but this destiny was forfeited through the free decision to sin. Through the incarnation, God restores man to his prelapsarian state as the believer participates in God through

50. *Autol.* 2.27, *ANF* 2:105.

51. Ibid. 2.16, *ANF* 2:101.

52. Ibid., 1.1 *ANF* 2:89.

53. Ibid., 1.7 *ANF* 2:91.

54. Ibid.

55. Kharlamov, "Deification in the Apologists," 79.

faith. The two primary benefits of union with God are immortality and incorruptibility. Although philosophically oriented, all three of these apologists argue for an economic form of theosis rather than the neoplatonic version that arises in later patristic theology.

Irenaeus

Irenaeus was the first proper theologian of the church in the post-Apostolic era, for the depth of his theological thought surpasses that of the Apostolic Fathers and early apologists of the church. Irenaeus expounds upon many themes already discussed in connection with various other figures, but notably places them into a broader theological and redemptive historical context.[56]

The first point to be noted is that Irenaeus' theology is Christocentric. In line with Ignatius, Irenaeus teaches a clear doctrine of the divine nature of Christ. He confesses, "He [Jesus] is God (for the name Emmanuel dictates this)."[57] Jesus "is Himself the Word of God."[58] He is the one "by whom all things were made"[59] since he is "the Creator of the world."[60] In a similar vein, Irenaeus writes that "there is one Almighty God, who made all things by His Word, both visible and invisible; showing at the same time, that by the Word, through whom God made the creation, He also bestowed

56. Finch summarizes Irenaeus' thought on theosis well writing: "Although he never employed the language of theopoiesis or theosis, already present in the theology of Irenaeus are all the essential elements of what would come to be regarded as the characteristically patristic understanding of sanctification as divinization: restoration of prelapsarian likeness to God and incorruptibility, initiated by the union of human nature with the divine nature through the incarnation, life, death, and resurrection of the Eternal Son, appropriated existentially as adoption by God and infusion by the Holy Spirit, and finally perfected eternally through the face to face vision of God" (Finch, "Christological Basis of Human Divinization," 86–87).

57. *Haer.* 3.21.4, *ANF* 1:452.

58. Ibid. 1.9.3, *ANF* 1:329.

59. Ibid. 1.9.2, *ANF* 1:329.

60. Ibid.

salvation on the men included in the creation."[61] Thus, Christ, as God, is the instrument of both creation and salvation.[62]

Not only does Jesus participate in divine activities, such as creation and redemption,[63] he is also the means by which God is known.[64] As Irenaeus explains, "God has been declared through the Son, who is in the Father, and has the Father in Himself—He who is, the Father bearing witness to the Son, and the Son announcing the Father."[65] Commensurate with this approach, Irenaeus writes: "the Father is the invisible of the Son, but the Son is the visible of the Father."[66]

The content of the Christian faith takes Christological shape in Irenaeus' theology. In a statement that serves as a summary of the Christian faith, Irenaeus confesses:

> Carefully preserving the ancient tradition, believing in one God, the Creator of heaven and earth, and all things therein, by means of Christ Jesus, the Son of God; who, because of His surpassing love towards His creation, condescended to be born of the virgin, He Himself uniting man through Himself to God, and having suffered under Pontius Pilate, and rising again, having been received up in splendor, shall come in glory, the Saviour of those who are saved, and the Judge of those who are judged, and

61. Ibid. 3.11.1, *ANF* 1:426.

62. In another instance, he writes that "God, then, was made man, and the Lord did Himself save us, giving us the token of the Virgin" (ibid. 3.21.1, *ANF* 1:451).

63. See, for example: "There is one Almighty God, who made all things by His Word, both visible and invisible; showing at the same time, that by the Word, through whom God made the creation, He also bestowed salvation on the men included in the creation" (ibid., 3.11.1, *ANF* 1:426).

64. "For He, the Son who is in His bosom, declares to all the Father who is invisible. Wherefore they know Him to whom the Son reveals Him; and again, the Father, by means of the Son, gives knowledge of His Son to those who love Him" (ibid.).

65. Ibid. 3.6.2, *ANF* 1:419.

66. Ibid. 4.6.6, *ANF* 1:469. He also writes similarly, "the Son is the knowledge of the Father; but the knowledge of the Son is in the Father, and has been revealed through the Son" (ibid. 4.6.7, *ANF* 1:469).

> sending into eternal fire those who transform the truth,
> and despise His Father and His advent.[67]

The narrative of Christ's life is referred to by Irenaeus as the "ancient tradition" that was passed down from the Apostles to the succeeding generations of Christians. The essence of the Christian message consists of Jesus' virgin birth, incarnation, death, resurrection, ascension, and return. So it is that those who reject Christ, and consequently the Father, will be judged.

Salvation, in Irenaeus' thought, is primarily placed in the category of recapitulation, which Quasten calls "the heart of Irenaeus' Christology and indeed of his entire theology."[68] In this incarnation-centric soteric model, it is proposed that God became man so that he might recapitulate the life of humanity within himself, and through that life, sanctify humanity.[69] Irenaeus writes:

> For He came to save all through means of Himself—all, I say, who through Him are born again to God—infants, and children, and boys, and youths, and old men. He therefore passed through every age, becoming as infant for infants, thus sanctifying infants; a child for children, thus sanctifying those who are of this age, being at the same time made to them an example of piety, righteousness, and submission; a youth for youths, becoming an example to youths, and thus sanctifying them for the Lord. So likewise He was an old man for old men, that He might be a perfect Master for all, not merely as respects the setting forth of truth, but also as regards age, sanctifying at

67. Ibid. 3.4.2, *ANF* 1:417.

68. Quasten, *Patrology*, 1:295.

69. Wingren defines recapitulation as "the accomplishment of God's plan of salvation, and this accomplishment is within history, in a time-sequence, and is not an episode at one particular point of time. It is a continuous process in which the οἰκονομία, *disposition*, of God is manifested by degrees. First, and most important of all—and the basis of our whole salvation—is the event of the birth of Jesus when the Son of God became an actual man. Many other things are consequent on this basic fact—the conflict, death, and Resurrection of Christ—but from one aspect what follows the primary event is simply a development of the resources of the power which was brought into the world through the child in Bethlehem" (Wingren, *Man and the Incarnation*, 81).

the same time the aged also, and becoming an example to them likewise. Then, at last, He came on to death itself, that He might be "the first-born from the dead, that in all things He might have the pre-eminence," the Prince of life, existing before all, and going before all.[70]

In Irenaeus' estimation, Christ lived a full human life, having passed through all stages of human existence so that each stage of life might be made holy. This is placed within an Adam-Christ contrast, as Paul discusses in Rom 5. For Irenaeus, all mankind fell in Adam, corrupting the human nature. Christ came to earth as a second Adam, restoring that which Adam had ruined through sin. Irenaeus contends that "as by one man's disobedience sin entered, and death obtained [a place] through sin; so also by the obedience of one man, righteousness having been introduced, shall cause life to fructify in those persons who in times past were dead."[71] The most notable aspect of the fall, for Irenaeus, is the reality of death. He states: "For the Lord, having been born 'the First-begotten of the dead,' and receiving into His bosom the ancient fathers, has regenerated them into the life God, He having been made Himself the beginning of those that live, as Adam became the beginning of those who die."[72] Through Adam, physical death came upon the human race as spiritual life was forfeited.[73] In Christ, both spiritual and physical death are overcome through the incarnation, cross, and resurrection.

---

70. *Haer.* 2.22.4, *ANF* 1:391.

71. Ibid. 3.21.10, *ANF* 1:454.

72. Ibid. 3.22.4, *ANF* 1:455.

73. Irenaeus sees Adam's fault not in his desire to be like God, but in his attempt to do so apart from God's means of deification. As Finch observes, "Thus, it was not Adam's aspiring to live a divine life, to be God-like, that he sinned, but in his succumbing to the temptation of egoism, that is, in attempting to acquire the glory of immortality and incorruptibility as his own autonomous possession rather than as a gift received from Another" (Finch, "Irenaeus on the Christological," 88).

Incarnation

For Irenaeus, the incarnation is the primary redemptive act in Christ's life. In line with our proposal of Christification, Irenaeus places deification within the context of the incarnation of the Second Person of the Holy Trinity. He argues that God and man, once separated by the fall, needed an act by which they could be united by a singular person. This act occurred through Christ's incarnation:

> And again: unless it had been God who had freely given salvation, we could never have possessed it securely. And unless man had been joined to God, he could never have become a partaker of incorruptibility. For it was incumbent upon the Mediator between God and men, by His relationship to both, to bring both to friendship and concord, and present man to God, while He revealed God to man. For, in what way could we be partaken of the adoption of sons, unless we had received from Him through the Son that fellowship which refers to Himself, unless His Word, having been made flesh, had entered into communion with us? Wherefore also He passed through every stage of life, restoring to all communion with God.[74]

Like the previous fathers examined here, Irenaeus places theosis within the context of communion with God, wherein the believer is restored to fellowship with the Creator and receives the divine quality of immortality. For Irenaeus, this is connected to the idea of recapitulation. Christ is not one person among many, but is instead the ideal human being through whom the destiny of the human race is decided. As he lives through each period of life, those stages of life are united with God and sanctified in turn. Through regeneration, the believer is adopted and engrafted into Christ, receiving his gift of human restoration.

Irenaeus argues that what happens to Christ also happens to those who identify with him through faith. He purports:

74. *Haer.* 2.22.4, *ANF* 1:391.

For as He became man in order to undergo temptation, so also was He the Word that He might be glorified; the Word remaining quiescent, that He might be
capable of being tempted, dishonoured, crucified, and of
suffering death, but the human nature being swallowed
up in it (the divine), when it conquered, and endured
[without yielding], and performed acts of kindness,
and rose again, and was received up [into heaven]. He
therefore, the Son of God, our Lord, being the Word of
the Father, and the Son of man, since He had a gen-
eration as to His human nature from Mary— who was
descended from mankind, and who was herself a human being— was made the Son of man. Wherefore also
the Lord Himself gave us a sign, in the depth below, and
in the height above, which man did not ask for, because
he never expected that a virgin could conceive, or that
it was possible that one remaining a virgin could bring
forth a son, and that what was thus born should be *God
with us*, and descend to those things which are of the
earth beneath, seeking the sheep which had perished.[75]

Jesus underwent temptation just as Adam underwent temptation. Adamic sin identified the human race with evil and death,
bringing both of these realities into the world. Christ reverses
these realities, bringing union with God. Adam was tempted in the
garden, where he gave in to the devil's lie. Christ is tempted by the
devil in the wilderness, recapitulating the temptation of Adam.[76]
In essence, "God recapitulated in Himself the ancient formation of
man, that He might kill sin, deprive death of its power, and vivify
man."[77] He took human nature upon himself so that he might both
take its corruption on himself through death, and raise it to glory
through the resurrection. Irenaeus writes similarly:

75. Ibid. 3.19.3, *ANF* 1:448.

76. "For He fought and conquered; for He was man contending for the
fathers, and through obedience doing away with disobedience completely: for
He bound the strong man, and set free the weak, and endowed His own handiwork with salvation, by destroying sin. For He is a most holy and merciful
Lord, and loves the human race" (ibid. 3.18.6, *ANF* 1:448).

77. Ibid. 3.18.7, *ANF* 1:448.

> when He became incarnate, and was made man, He commenced afresh the long line of human beings, and furnished us, in a brief, comprehensive manner, with salvation; so that what we had lost in Adam—namely, to be according to the image and likeness of God—that we might recover in Christ Jesus.

Thus, through Christ's person the corrupt Adamic nature is destroyed just as deified human nature is established.

Irenaeus' writing shows a consistent pattern of discord and harmony. The fall interrupted the unity inherent in creation, separating humans from one another and from their Creator. This disunity is also apparent in creation itself, for as Irenaeus states:

> There is therefore, as I have pointed out, one God the Father, and one Christ Jesus, who came by means of the whole dispensational arrangements [connected with Him], and gathered together all things in Himself. But in every respect, too, He is man, the formation of God; and thus He took up man into Himself, the invisible becoming visible, the incomprehensible being made comprehensible, the impassible becoming capable of suffering, and the Word being made man, thus summing up all things in Himself: so that as in super-celestial, spiritual, and invisible things, the Word of God is supreme, so also in things visible and corporeal He might possess the supremacy, and, taking to Himself the pre-eminence, as well as constituting Himself Head of the Church, He might draw all things to Himself at the proper time.[78]

In Jesus, the ultimate union of the transcendent and created realms is realized. Through Jesus, God is made manifest, humanity is made capable of incorruption, and the created realm is placed under the authority of Christ. This authority will realize itself at the eschatological consummation, when the unity that has begun in the postlapsarian period will be made manifest.

The incarnation was the only means by which humanity could partake in divine qualities. Irenaeus argues: "For by no other

---

78. Ibid. 3.16.6, *ANF* 1:443.

means could we have attained to incorruptibility and immortality, unless we had been united to incorruptibility and immortality."[79] There is clear participatory intent in Irenaeus' thought on this point. Humanity participates in divinity through the incarnation. This participation results in the transfer of divine qualities to the human race, which consists primarily of immortality and incorruptibility. Irenaeus asks,

> But how could we be joined to incorruptibility and immortality, unless, first, incorruptibility and immortality had become that which we also are, so that the corruptible might be swallowed up by incorruptibility, and the mortal by immortality, that we might receive the adoption of sons?[80]

The divine aspects of Christ's person overcome his human frailty. This should not be read as an early form of Eutychianism, wherein the human nature is erased due to the prominence of his divinity, but as the exaltation of his human nature through the unity of Christ's person. This anticipates the later Lutheran teaching on the *communicatio idiomatum*.

The reality of participation in divine attributes leads us to the question of the validity of distinguishing between God's essence and energies. Although he consistently speaks of participation in divine qualities, Irenaeus never differentiates God's essence from these qualities. [81] Finch astutely observes this fact, explaining that

79. Ibid. 3.19.1, *ANF* 1:448.

80. Ibid.

81. Finch argues: "How, if at all, did Irenaeus understand God's life and incorruptibility to be partakable by creatures while at the same time remaining singularly His own? Are they somehow external to His 'totally inaccessible' essence, as the neo-Palamite school of thought insists? Such a solution is insupportable from the textual evidence, at least in part because Irenaeus writes just as readily of human participation in God Himself and in the Holy Spirit and in the Son as he does of human participation in God's perfections, such as incorruptibility, freedom, light, glory, life, salvation, and wisdom" (Finch, "Irenaeus on the Christological," 93). Thus far, this is consistent with our observations that deification, for the early fathers, consists in the transfer of certain divine attributes through union with God. It is this view, rather than the Palamite understanding, that is reflected in Irenaeus.

"it does not appear that Irenaeus was here suggesting that God has withheld a distinct mode of Himself—His essence—from His otherwise immediate presence and generous self-disclosure to the world."[82] This leads Finch to conclude,

> The writings of Irenaeus cannot be marshaled to support the neo-Palamite position that the fathers of the Church grounded the possibility of sanctifying participation in God upon a real distinction between an intrinsically incommunicable divine essence and God's communicable energies. Irenaeus assumes and implies that the divine persons of the Holy Spirit and the Son are no less communicable than are the divine perfections which Irenaeus clearly locates within what he repeatedly insists is God's entirely simple essence.[83]

For Irenaeus, the incarnation reveals God himself, not simply his energies. This divine essence is inherently participatory through the indwelling Trinity.

One section of Irenaeus' writing speaks directly of humanity becoming gods, drawing upon the text from Ps 82. Irenaeus states,

> But, being ignorant of Him who from the Virgin is Emmanuel, they are deprived of His gift, which is eternal life; and not receiving the incorruptible Word, they remain in mortal flesh, and are debtors to death, not obtaining the antidote of life. To whom the Word says, mentioning His own gift of grace: "I said, You are all the sons of the Highest, and gods; but you shall die like men." He speaks undoubtedly these words to those who have not received the gift of adoption, but who despise the incarnation of the pure generation of the Word of God, defraud human nature of promotion into God, and prove themselves ungrateful to the Word of God, who became flesh for them. For it was for this end that the Word of God was made man, and He who was the Son of God became the Son of man, that man, having been taken into

82. Ibid., 95.
83. Ibid., 103.

the Word, and receiving the adoption, might become
the son of God.[84]

Irenaeus is here speaking of a distinction between the children of God and "those who have not received the gift of adoption." He identifies God's "gift of grace" with being "sons of the Highest" and "gods." Although the Word "became flesh for them," these individuals reject the deification that is truly offered to them through the incarnation of Christ. This rejection results in death, as well as a consequent lack of "promotion into God." Conversely, those who do believe the gospel are "taken into the Word" and "receive adoption" such that they might "become the sons of God." Irenaeus' language is clearly participatory, for he speaks of "promotion into God" as well as "being taken into the Word." This participation in God allows for Christians to themselves be called "gods," which likely runs parallel to his concept of adoption.

This quote also demonstrates that for Irenaeus, as for all of the fathers examined thus far, deification offers two primary benefits to the receiver: divine incorruptibility and immortality. At the beginning of this section, Irenaeus speaks of unbelievers as being "deprived of His gift, which is eternal life; and not receiving the incorruptible Word." Instead, unbelievers "remain in mortal flesh, and are debtors to death, not obtaining the antidote of life." God's gift of salvation is identified with the incorruptible Word and eternal life, signifying both incorruptibility and immortality. Instead, those who reject the gospel remain mortal, and are indebted to death.

All of the passages examined up to this point allow for a comprehensive theology of deification within the thought of Irenaeus. According to Irenaeus, humanity was created in the image and likeness of God for communion with the Triune persons. However, humanity rejected such communion through the fall, and thus lost the divine likeness. Instead of life and salvation, humanity headed toward death and rejection of God. Through the incarnation, God undid the damage caused by the fall. In the person of Christ, divine and human natures were united. This union is not simply a

84. *Haer.* 3.19.3, *ANF* 1:448–49.

personal reality that affected Christ as an individual, but one that fundamentally changed the relationship between God and his creation. Through Jesus, the ontological gap that separated God from humanity was bridged and fellowship was restored. Christians, through faith, become adopted as sons of God, and can even be called "gods." Christians participate in the divine nature, and through such participation, receive the divine attributes of incorruptibility and immortality.

The Cross

Critics may be tempted to argue that Irenaeus—in an unbiblical manner—places soteriology within the realm of the incarnation to the exclusion of the cross and resurrection, which are central in Paul's theology. Irenaeus does, however, write frequently about the salvific nature of the cross. Indeed, he writes that "Christ did suffer, and was Himself the Son of God, who died for us, and redeemed us with His blood."[85] In this way, the cross of Christ is itself an instrument of redemption, not the incarnation alone. In a more comprehensive statement, Irenaeus writes:

> Jesus Christ, the Son of God, is one and the same, who did by suffering reconcile us to God, and rose from the dead; who is at the right hand of the Father, and perfect in all things . . . For He did Himself truly bring in salvation: since He is Himself the Word of God, Himself the Only-begotten of the Father, Christ Jesus our Lord. [86]

As demonstrated above, Irenaeus speaks of the reconciliation of humanity occurring through the incarnation, by which the ontological gap that exists between God and man was overcome. However, in this passage it becomes apparent that the incarnation *itself* was not capable of such reconciliation. The cross is also a necessary act of God, wherein the Adamic curse of death is defeated through Christ's atonement. Similarly, Irenaeus writes that

85. Ibid. 33.16.9, *ANF* 1:444.
86. Ibid.

Christ "redeemed us from apostasy with His own blood, so that we should also be sanctified people."[87] Sanctification is thus also a benefit of the cross.

Daniel Wilson argues that a form of substitutionary atonement in Irenaeus' thought underlies his approach to deification. Wilson writes: "Christ's work on the cross fulfills the requirements for the payment of humanity's sin debt, and his atonement is the climax of his Incarnation, which provides the means by which humanity may unite with him and receive deification."[88] This juridical aspect of Irenaeus' theology is demonstrated by several texts within his writings. One section that is particularly clear is from the fifth book of Irenaeus' *Against Heresies*, in which he writes:

> Therefore, by remitting sins, He did indeed heal man, while He also manifested Himself who He was. For if no one can forgive sins but God alone, while the Lord remitted them and healed men, it is plain that He was Himself the Word of God made the Son of man, receiving from the Father the power of remission of sins; since He was man, and since He was God, in order that since as man He suffered for us, so as God He might have compassion on us, and forgive us our debts, in which we were made debtors to our Creator. And therefore David said beforehand, "Blessed are they whose iniquities are forgiven, and whose sins are covered. Blessed is the man to whom the Lord has not imputed sin;" pointing out thus that remission of sins which follows upon His advent, by which "He has destroyed the handwriting" of our debt, and "fastened it to the cross;" so that as by means of a tree we were made debtors to God, [so also] by means of a tree we may obtain the remission of our debt.[89]

Irenaeus seems comfortable using the language of "debt" in this context. He argues that mankind has been under a debt owed to God since the fall of Adam, and that by means of the "tree we were made debtors to God." This is not a ransom paid to Satan,

---

87. Ibid. 3.5.3, *ANF* 1:418.

88. Wilson, *Deification*, 55.

89. *Haer.* 5.17.3, *ANF* 1:545.

for the context makes it clear that "we were made debtors to our Creator." Through the cross, Christ pays the debt that humanity owes. This understanding is made clear by the parallel Irenaeus draws between the two trees. The first tree brings humanity into debt; the second tree remits humanity's debt.[90] The forgiveness of sins is a necessary aspect of humanity's deification. In order for humanity to be united to God, sin needs to be dealt with. This occurs through the cross, where Christ takes this debt upon himself.[91] Thus, it becomes apparent that juridical language is not opposed to participationist themes in Irenaeus' thought. Salvation includes both ontological union with God through the incarnation and the remission of sins through the vicarious atonement of Christ.

The resurrection is also an essential aspect of Irenaeus' soteriology. He does not view the resurrection as redemptive simply as a demonstration that the cross was efficacious, but argues instead that the resurrection itself affects salvation. He purports:

> [Jesus] offering and commending to His Father that human nature (*hominem*) which had been found, making in His own person the first-fruits of the resurrection of man; that, as the Head rose from the dead, so also the remaining part of the body—[namely, the body] of everyman who is found in life—when the time is fulfilled of that condemnation which existed by reason of disobedience, may arise, blended together and strengthened through means of joints and bands by the increase of God, each of the members having its own proper and fit position in the body. For there are many mansions in the Father's house, inasmuch as there are also many members in the body.[92]

90. Wilson notes, "Irenaeus consistently links the redemptive aspect of the tree with Christ's obedience as payment directly to God for the debt incurred by humanity" (Wilson, *Deification*, 54–55).

91. "Humanity's deification called for re-creation of the image and likeness. For this re-creation to occur, Christ, the true Image and Likeness, had to pay the penalty of death that humanity incurred due to its sin. Therefore, Christ took humanity's place and became the vicarious sacrifice to atone for the sins of humanity and re-create the skewed image and likeness" (ibid., 51).

92. *Haer.* 3.19.3, *ANF* 1:448.

Since Irenaeus speaks of Christ taking on the nature, not only of a single individual, but of the entire human race, he believes that which happens to Jesus becomes the destiny of humanity. Just as Christ's sanctified human existence sanctifies each stage of life, Jesus' resurrection assures and inaugurates the resurrection of the human race. Through identification with Christ, the identity of Jesus becomes that of his people, and they share in his Sonship and sanctification as well as in his resurrection from the dead.

Though it would be unwarranted to argue for a doctrine of *sola fide* in Irenaeus, he is clear to state that redemption, including deification, is an act of grace. He confesses, "we see, that not by ourselves, but by the help of God, we must be saved."[93] Speaking of those in the old covenant, Irenaeus is quick to state, "it was the Lord Himself who saved them, because they could not be saved by their own instrumentality."[94] Similarly, Irenaeus purports that "the 'good thing' of our salvation is not from us, but from God."[95] Irenaeus' concept of deification is thus not a moralistic one, but is in fact thoroughly grounded in God's grace, especially as shown through the incarnation of Christ.

Indeed, faith is central to Irenaeus' thought. He confesses that God "makes those that believe in His name the sons of God . . . For it is He who descended and ascended for the salvation of men."[96] Those "who acknowledge His Son's advent"[97] are rendered "perfect towards God."[98] Along with Paul, Irenaeus uses the example of Abraham to demonstrate the importance of faith: "The Lord, therefore, was not unknown to Abraham, whose day he desired to see; nor, again, was the Lord's Father, for he had learned from the Word of the Lord, and believed Him; wherefore it was accounted to him by the Lord for righteousness. For faith towards

---

93. Ibid. 3.20.3, *ANF* 1:450.
94. Ibid.
95. Ibid.
96. Ibid. 3.6.2, *ANF* 1:419.
97. Ibid. 3.12.5, *ANF* 1:432.
98. Ibid.

God justifies a man."[99] In this way, the Christian is justified by faith, which is counted as righteousness before God. Faith receives not only righteousness, but also the blessings of union with God, such as incorruptibility and immortality. Irenaeus argues that "for this purpose did the Father reveal the Son, that through His instrumentality He might be manifested to all, and might receive those righteous ones who believe in Him into incorruption and everlasting enjoyment."[100] However, it must be noted that Irenaeus qualifies this statement by writing, "to believe in Him is to do His will."[101] Thus, while Irenaeus may adopt a *form* of *sola fide*, he includes obedience within his definition of faith.

Irenaeus also makes it apparent that the law is not an instrument of salvation, but that the law shows sin and brings about death, pointing toward the necessity of the incarnation, death, and resurrection of Christ:

> But the law coming, which was given by Moses, and testifying of sin that it is a sinner, did truly take away his (death's) kingdom, showing that he was no king, but a robber; and it revealed him as a murderer. It laid, however, a weighty burden upon man, who had sin in himself, showing that he was liable to death. For as the law was spiritual, it merely made sin to stand out in relief, but did not destroy it. For sin had no dominion over the spirit, but over man. For it behooved Him who was to destroy sin, and redeem man under the power of death, that He should Himself be made that very same thing which he was, that is, man; who had been drawn by sin into bondage, but was held by death, so that sin should be destroyed by man, and man should go forth from death. For as by the disobedience of the one man who was originally moulded from virgin soil, the many were made sinners, and forfeited life; so was it necessary that, by the obedience of one man, who was

99. Ibid. 4.5.5, *ANF* 1:467.
100. Ibid. 4.6.5, *ANF* 1:469.
101. Ibid.

originally born from a virgin, many should be justified and receive salvation.[102]

The law did not offer salvation, but merely demonstrated to humanity that all were held under corruption and death. Sin needed to be destroyed by a human, but this could not be done by mere obedience to the law, since all humankind was under its curse. Jesus therefore became a man so that he might defeat sin and conquer death. The obedience of Christ reverses the disobedience of Adam, and through his person, both justification and salvation are granted.

Conclusion

Irenaeus' view of theosis can rightly be labeled "Christification." In his view, Christ's incarnation came as a necessary result of sin. Adam destined the human race for death and corruption. These and other effects of sin needed to be conquered so that the human race could share in incorruption. For this reason, God became incarnate in the person of Jesus Christ so that sin and death could be defeated. Jesus recapitulated the life of Adam, sanctifying the human race and restoring the relationship between God and man. Through faith, the Christian participates in God and receives the benefits of Christ's life, death, and resurrection, which are primarily identified with immortality and incorruptibility. There is also an important judicial element to Irenaeus' thought, wherein Christ pays the debt of human sin upon the cross. In this way, theosis is a result of grace, not of human effort. The law demonstrated to humankind that deification could not be achieve by human obedience and pointed to the one whose obedience restored fellowship between God and his creation.

102. Ibid. 3.18.7, *ANF* 1:448.

Athanasius

Athanasius' soteriology is essentially an expansion upon that of Irenaeus. For Athanasius, the fall consisted of the loss of union with God and the penalty of death. These two results of Adam's sin are resolved through Christ, who came as the second Adam. Through his incarnation, Jesus overcame the metaphysical barrier that separated God and man. God became man so that man might become God. Death was overcome through Jesus' death, wherein he bore the penalty of sin upon his own body. Athanasius' soteriology is at once legal and ontological; sinners are saved from the penalty of their sin even as they are restored to divine fellowship.

The fall, in Athanasius' thought, has a twofold effect. First, it results in a distorted relationship between God and man, and second, it results in death. Athanasius writes:

> Thus, then, God has made man, and willed that he should abide in incorruption; but men, having despised and rejected the contemplation of God, and devised and contrived evil for themselves . . . received the condemnation of death from which they had been threatened; and from thenceforth no longer remained as they were made, but were being corrupted according to their devices; and death had the mastery over them as king.[103]

The two themes that have arisen in all of the literature examined thus far are immortality and incorruption. Athanasius likewise discusses these two aspects of creation and redemption; he argues that God created humankind to participate in these gifts. Humanity was to contemplate God, participate in divine fellowship, and receive the divine blessings of incorruption and eternal life. The fall results in the loss of these gifts. Humanity departed from their created purpose, falling into sin and receiving corruption and death.

In Athanasius' thought, the image of God is retained in humankind, but became so distorted as to be in danger of being lost. He argues that "the rational man in God's image was disappearing,

103. *Inc.* 4, *NPNF*2 4:38.

and the handiwork of God was in process of dissolution."[104] This image is restored through the incarnation. Athanasius purports, "whereas men had turned toward corruption, He might turn them again toward incorruption, and quicken them from death by the appropriation of His body and by the grace of the Resurrection, banishing death from them like straw from the fire."[105] The reception of incorruption, an essential aspect of theosis for the early church, comes through both the incarnation and resurrection. At his resurrection, Jesus put on an incorruptible body, and in turn gave incorruptibility to all who belong to him. Through his resurrection from death, Jesus "made a new beginning of life for us."[106]

Athanasius famously argues, "He was made man that we might be made God; and He manifested Himself in a body that we might receive the idea of the unseen Father; and He endured the insolence of men that we might inherit immortality."[107] This is an explicit statement of theosis that is connected to the incarnation of God and the gift of divine immortality through union with him. Athanasius' doctrine of theosis is Christification, because any discussion of man's elevation into participation with divinity is rooted in the incarnation. Through the incarnation, Athanasius writes, "He put on a body, that He might find death in the body, and blot it out."[108] Death served as a hindrance, capturing humanity under its spell so that immortality could not be achieved. The reality of death was taken away through Christ's atonement. This death served to bring about theosis, or in other words, "for our sakes He is dishonoured, that we may be brought to honour."[109]

Both the deity and humanity of Christ are necessary for humanity's deification. Athanasius argues that "none other could create anew the likeness of God's image in men, save the Image of the Father; and . . . none other could render the mortal immortal,

104. Ibid. 6, *NPNF*2 4:39.
105. Ibid. 8, *NPNF*2 4:40.
106. Ibid. 10.5, *NPNF*2 4:41.
107. Ibid. 54.3, *NPNF*2 4:65.
108. Ibid. 44.6, *NPNF*2 4:60.
109. Ibid. 34.3, *NPNF*2 4:54.

save our Lord Jesus Christ, Who is the Very Life."[110] So it is that
the transference of the divine image is initiated by the Father, who
reflects his own glory perfectly in the Son; the image of the Son
is then reflected—in an imperfect manner—in his creation. This
demonstrates a consistent pattern in Athanasius' thought that divine blessings are initiated by the Father and enacted through the
Son and Spirit.

A strong strand of legal language is apparent in Athanasius.
He argues that sin puts humanity under a legal debt that must be
paid. He claims, "For death, as I said above, gained from that time
forth a legal hold over us, and it was impossible to evade the law,
since it had been laid down by God because of the transgression,
and the result was in truth at once monstrous and unseemly."[111]
This debt must be paid in order for God to be just, and therefore
God came into the world to pay that debt on behalf of humankind:
"For being over all, the Word of God naturally by offering His own
temple and corporeal instrument for the life of all satisfied the debt
by His death."[112] The cross, for Athanasius, is a vicarious act. Jesus
became man so that he might pay the debt of death than all humankind owes to God, cancelling what was owed by all humanity.
Athanasius often uses the language of law along with that of debt.
For example, Athanasius writes, "by the sacrifice of His own body,
He both put an end to the law which was against us, and made a
new beginning of life for us, by the hope of resurrection which He
has given us."[113] This act of sacrifice was the only means of salvation, because "the race of men had gone to ruin, had not the Lord
and Saviour of all, the Son of God, come among us to meet the end
of death."[114] In this way, Jesus' death is a sacrifice for all people.
Athanasius argues that "the death of all was accomplished in the
Lord's body, and that death and corruption were wholly done away

110. Ibid. 20.1 *NPNF2* 4:47.
111. Ibid. 6, *NPNF2* 4:39.
112. Ibid. 9.2, *NPNF2* 4:41.
113. Ibid. 10.5, *NPNF2* 4:41.
114. Ibid. 9.4, *NPNF2* 4:41.

with by reason of the Word that was united with it."[115] The Word, in uniting with flesh, united himself with the entire human race, thus achieving on behalf of humanity comprehensively. Consequently, the death of Christ was the death of all sin. This was necessary because "death must needs be suffered on behalf of all, that the debt owing from all might be paid."[116] Again, this is a vicarious act through which Christ pays off the debt that is owed by all sinners, although he himself remains innocent.

There are several sections in Athanasius' writing where it becomes apparent that the legal and participationist aspects of his soteriology cohere with one another. Athanasius writes, "the most holy Son of the Father, being the Image of the Father, came to our region to renew man once made in His likeness, and find him, as one lost, by the remission of sins."[117] The remission of sins is the means by which the divine likeness can be restored. Sin is a barrier to theosis, and thus the guilt of sin must be overcome for the divine image to be restored. In this model, the death and resurrection of Christ hold together as two necessary aspects of one redemptive act. Through death, the penalty of sin is paid and sins are remitted; through the resurrection, the image of God is restored and new life dispensed. Thus, the Savior's work consists in "putting away death from us and renewing us again."[118] Again, Athanasius includes the forensic and metaphysical aspects of redemption together as parts of a comprehensive soteriology, writing:

> But since it was necessary also that the debt owing from all should be paid again: for, as I have already said, it was owing that all should die, for which a special cause indeed, He came among us: to this intent, after the proofs of His Godhead from His works, He next offered up His sacrifice also on behalf of all, yielding His Temple to death in the stead of all, firstly to make men quit and free of their old trespasses, and further to shew Himself more

115. Ibid. 20.5, *NPNF2* 4:47.
116. Ibid.
117. Ibid. 14.2, *NPNF2* 4:43.
118. Ibid. 16.5 *NPNF2* 4:45.

powerful even than death, displaying His own body incorruptible, as first-fruits of the resurrection of all.[119]

Through Adam's sin, all humans owe a debt of death to God.
This debt needed to be paid for God to justly redeem humanity.
Jesus then took this debt upon himself, receiving the punishment
that all deserved. Yet atonement is not limited to this vicarious
model, but also includes the restoration of the human person as
incorruptible through the resurrection of Christ. Jesus' resurrected
body is, then, the means by which all of humanity can participate in God through the incorruption each receives at their own
resurrection.

In Athanasius, the "Anselmian" and *Christus Victor* motifs
cohere with one another. He argues that Christ:

> took to Himself a body such as could die, that He might
> offer it as His own in the stead of all, and as suffering,
> through His union with it, on behalf of all, "Bring to
> nought Him that had the power of death, that is the
> devil; and might deliver them who through fear of death
> were all their lifetime subject to bondage."[120]

In this statement, Athanasius speaks of Christ as a substitute
who died "in the stead of all." Even as Christ pays the debt owed
by the human race, he also defeats the works of the devil, freeing
humans from spiritual bondage. This demonstrates that the false
dichotomy proposed by both Protestant and Eastern interpreters
has no grounding in the writings of Athanasius. In Athanasius, as
well as other patristic sources, legal and ontological categories coexist in perfect harmony. The contemporary church would do well
to rediscover this patristic model.

Conclusion

There are several commonalities between all of the figures ex-
plored above. For Ignatius, Irenaeus, Justin, and Athanasius, the

119. Ibid. 20.2, *NPNF2* 4:47.
120. Ibid. 20.6, *NPNF2* 4:47.

theme of deification is Christological. All soteriological blessings are achieved through Christ, and deification comes chiefly through the act of the incarnation. This incarnation-centric theology does not ignore the acts of death and resurrection, but utilizes all three redemptive realities in a multifaceted doctrine of salvation. For many of these writers, a belief in theosis does not negate the importance of the forgiveness of sins or the legal nature of atonement. Irenaeus and Athanasius boldly proclaim a doctrine of substitutionary atonement that coincides with their emphasis on both deification and the *Christus Victor* motif. Finally, deification is not, for these writers, an abstract philosophical reality. Rather, it is an economic reality, placed within the scope of the divine *oikonomia* that is principally explained as the transfer of divine immortality and incorruptibility through union with God.

5

The Neoplatonic Approach to Deification

Dionysius the Areopagite

THE SECOND PRIMARY STREAM of thought regarding deification is popularized through the writings of Pseudo-Dionysius the Areopagite. In opposition to the economic approach to theosis, the Dionysian perspective is speculative and philosophical, rooted as it is in a Christian revision of neoplatonic philosophy. The Areopagite's teachings were popularized in the East by Maximus the Confessor and Gregory Palamas, and in the West by Johannes Scotus Eriugena, who translated the Areopagite's writings into Latin in the ninth century. His influence survives in the Eastern Church, especially in the Neopalamite tradition. The two primary distinctions between the Dionysian and earlier patristic approaches are in the realm of apophaticism and mystical experience. For Dionysius, God's essence is unknowable. Divine transcendence negates the usefulness of positive affirmation about God, including his biblical titles. Positive affirmation can only achieve an approximate knowledge of God. God's utter transcendence means that he is beyond anything which can be named. Thus, for Dionysius, God can be best known through mystical experience, by which the believer has a direct encounter with the supreme reality that cannot be described in human language. This idea would later be expounded upon by a distinction between God's essence and energies. Though God's essence remains hidden to human perception and experience, his energies are interactive and participatory.

The author of the Dionysian writings remains anonymous. He writes under the pseudonym of the Areopagite who was converted by Saint Paul (Acts 17:34). It is universally accepted that this attribution is invalid, due to the influence of later neoplatonic thinking on his thought and the lack of citation prior to the sixth century. Although there is no scholarly consensus on the identity of the author, it is generally agreed that his writings appeared in the late fifth to early sixth century. The citations of neoplatonic philosopher Proclus, who died in AD 485, preclude a pre-fifth century dating. The influence of Proclus apparent in these writings has led some scholars to believe that Dionysius was himself a student of Proclus, although this cannot be verified.

Dionysius distinguishes between two means of approaching theology. The first, positive theology, is based upon affirmative statements about deity. The knowledge that this type of method can gain, according to Dionysius, is approximate and imperfect. He argues that the better form of theological discussion is apophatic, or negative. This manner of theological discourse proceeds by way of negation—a discussion of what God *is not*. As Dionysius explains:

> Now we must wholly distinguish this negative method from that of positive statements. For, when we were making positive statements, and then through intermediate terms we came to particular titles, but now ascending upwards from particular to universal conceptions, we strip off all qualities in order that we may attain a naked knowledge of that Unknowing, which in all existant things is enwrapped by all objects of knowledge, and that we may begin to see that super-essential Darkness which is hidden by all the light that is in existent things.[1]

The goal in Dionysian theology is to gain an experiential knowledge of God that is divorced from concrete theological statements regarding the divine essence. The being and attributes of God transcend explanation, and thus can be best known without explanation. Through contemplation with the *via negativa*, the

---

1. Dionysius, *Divine Names and the Mystical Theology*, ch. 2.

believer may begin to know God in a manner that transcends thought and language.

The divine essence transcends the various biblical names and attributes which are applied to divinity. The Areopogite's treatise, *The Divine Names*, expounds upon the various names attached to God in Scripture and puts forth the argument that none of these names captures God's essential character, but the divine transcends such linguistic limitations. Dionysius refers to God as "the Unutterable and Nameless Godhead."[2] In a statement which summarizes Dionysius' approach to divine attributes he writes:

> For we make no promise to express the Absolute Super-Essential Goodness and Being and Life and Wisdom of the Absolute Super-Essential Godhead which (as saith the Scripture) hath Its foundation in a secret place beyond all Goodness, Godhead, Being, Wisdom, and Life; but we are considering the benignant Providence which is revealed to us and are celebrating It as Transcendent Goodness and Cause of all good things, and as Existent as Life and as Wisdom, and as productive Cause of Existence of Life and the Giver of Wisdom, in those creatures which partake of Existence, Life, Intelligence, and Perception.[3]

Although he states that the divine reality is beyond all "Godhead," Dionysius does accept the doctrine of the Trinity as a revealed truth, and thus does not seek to argue that Trinitarian language is completely unworthy of the divine essence.[4] However, he confesses that "all Divine things, even those that are revealed

---

2. Ibid., 1:8.

3. Ibid., 5:2.

4. At times, Dionysius does imply that God transcends Trinity: "But no Unity or Trinity or Number or Oneness or Fecundity or any other thing that either is a creature or can be known to any creature, is able to utter the mystery, beyond all mind and reason, of that Transcendent Godhead which super-essentially surpasses all things. It hath no name, nor can it be grasped by reason; It dwells in a region beyond us, where our feet cannot tread. Even the title of 'Goodness' we do not ascribe to It because we think such a name unsuitable" (ibid, 13:3).

to us, are only known by their communications. Their ultimate nature, which they possess in their own original being, is beyond Mind and beyond all Being and knowledge."[5] For Dionysius, unity has priority over multiplicity, although even the category of unity is transcended by the divine essence.[6] He argues that "in divine things the undifferenced Unities are of more might that the Differentiations and hold the foremost place and retain their state of Undifference even after the One has, without departing from Its oneness, entered into Differentiation."[7] Dionysius' emphasis on unity over differentiation caused Johannes Scotus Eriugena to argue that differentiation within the Trinity is only apparent, and that behind Trinitarian manifestation is a supreme unity. Though Dionysius himself does not arrive at such a conclusion, it is a danger inherent in his approach.

For Dionysius, reality is inherently participatory. All of creation exists in participation with God. He elaborates this idea using an analogy between God and the sun, explaining:

> For as our sun, through no choice or deliberation, but by the very fact of its existence, gives light to all those things which have any inherent power of sharing its illumination, even so the Good (which is above the sun, as the transcendent archetype by the very mode of its existence is above its faded image) sends forth upon all things according to their receptive powers, the rays of Its undivided Goodness.[8]

So it is that God, by his very nature, is participatory, and reality always participates in his being in order that it too might have being. Due to his participationist ontology, Dionysius accepts the common neoplatonic attribution of evil as a privation. That

---

5. Ibid. 2:7.

6. "He is an Unity in a manner far different from this, above all unity which is in the world; yea, He is an Indivisible Plurality, insatiable yet brim-full, producing, perfecting, and maintaining all unity and plurality" (ibid. 2:11).

7. Ibid.

8. Ibid. 4:1.

which is good participates in divinity.[9] The less good something is, the less it participates in God's being. Utter evil is tantamount to nonexistence.[10]

Deification is expounded upon within the realm of this participationist ontology. Dionysius frequently speaks of theosis, confessing, "with undeviating power He gives Himself for the Deification of those that turn to Him."[11] Dionysius does not place deification, as earlier writers do, primarily in the context of the divine economy. Though Dionysius cites Scripture frequently, he does not expound upon the historical events of Christ's life as the primary means of deification. In Athanasius and Irenaeus, theosis is an economic reality that explains what happened to humanity through the incarnation and resurrection of Christ, wherein God's attributes of immortality and incorruptibility are granted to those who unite themselves to God by faith. It is chiefly a redemptive historical category, and the experience of theosis occurs through the sacramental life of the church and human suffering, whereby Christians participate in Christ's sufferings. For Dionysius, theosis occurs through mystical experience, wherein the believer encounters the nameless Absolute. He writes:

> I counsel that, in the earnest exercise of mystic contemplation, thou leave the senses and the activities of the intellect and all things that the senses or the intellect can perceive, and all things in this world of nothingness, or in that world of being, and that, thine understanding being laid to rest, thou strain (so far as thou mayest) towards an union with Him whom neither being nor understanding can contain.[12]

---

9. "Or rather, to speak shortly, all creatures in so far as they have being are good and come from the Good, and in so far as they are deprived of the Good, neither are good nor have they being" (ibid. 2:20).

10. "And, in a word, evil (as we have often sais) is weakness, impotence, and deficiency of knowledge (or, at least, of exercised knowledge), or of faith, desire, or activity as touching the good" (ibid. 4:35).

11. Ibid. 9:5.

12. Ibid., ch. 1.

Through the *via negativa*, the believer can achieve a state of ecstatic union wherein the Christian encounters the Absolute in an experience that exceeds thought and language. The Dionysian approach to theotic experience mirrors that of neoplatonic philosophy in many ways.[13] His concern is with God as a being, rather than with the historical events of redemption. The neoplatonist philosopher Plotinus similarly argues that God is to be known by way of negation, and unification with the One.[14] Like Plotinus, Dionysius seeks to gain an understanding of that which is unknowable through mystical experience. This results in an explanation of the issue of the one and the many, with all things originating in one source and eventually returning to that source.[15]

The Experience of Deification

A primary aspect of the Eastern understanding of theosis, which differentiates it from the earlier economic strand of teaching, is the way in which theosis is achieved through mystical experience. This experiential approach to theosis arises from Dionysius' writings, but is especially developed in the writings and practice of Gregory Palamas. Palamas founded a movement known as Hesychasm (ἡσυχασμός). The Hesychasts emphasized the experience of the divine through silent contemplation and repetition of the Jesus Prayer. Through these mystical practices, the Hesychasts claimed to experience the "uncreated light" which was identical to that light seen by the Apostles at Mount Tabor. This light was said to be an experience of the divine energies, as opposed to the divine essence. This idea was attacked by Barlaam of Seminara, who argued that to purport a distinction between essence and energies in God

13. Lossky correctly points out that there are important differences between Plotinus and Dionysius (*Mystical Theology*, 30–33). However, despite the differences Lossky demonstrates, I am still convinced that neoplatonism informs Dionysius' mysticism more than the text of the New Testament.

14. See Lenz, "Deification of the Philosopher," 47–67.

15. For a full explanation of Dionysius' place within the neoplatonic tradition, see Perl, *Theophany*.

is to become a polytheist, creating two distinct aspects of God: one unknowable, and one knowable. Palamas' view was affirmed in numerous church councils and has generally been accepted within the Eastern Orthodox tradition.

In Palamas' approach, the experience of deification is achieved primarily through prayer, although it is also aided by the good works of believers. In prayer, the believer elevates himself toward God, rising above the sensible temporal world. Palamas' discussion of the nature of "perpetual prayer" which is commanded in 1 Thessalonians,[16] was highly influential in the Eastern tradition. Palamas argues that incessant prayer "is nothing if not the perpetual and living communion of man with God, made possible when man receives within himself the gift of prayer."[17] This act of incessant prayer has ascetical import. As believers deprive themselves of temporal good through ascetic acts, their souls are prepared to cooperate with God through the gift of incessant prayer.[18]

An important form of prayer that Palamas urged the Hesychasts to engage in is known as the "psychosomatic method of prayer," which is done through repetition of the Jesus prayer: "Lord Jesus Christ, Son of God, have mercy on me a sinner," or simply the phrase, "Lord Jesus." The Hesychasts often prayed this way for hours at a time, holding their chins to their chest and staring at their navels. The goal of such a practice is to unite the intellect and the heart. In such a union, the believer's "heart [is] purified of all passion" while the "intellect [is] emptied of all care and thought."[19] Prayer is essential in the process of deification. Initially, prayer consists of spoken words that carry the Christian's individual petitions to God. This is active prayer. A higher form

16. "Pray without ceasing" (1 Thess 5:17).

17. Mantzaridēs, *Deification of Man*, 91.

18. Palamas' approach to incessant prayer is formulated in contrast to Barlaam, who argued that "man prays incessantly once he has gained the habit of prayer. The habit of prayer, according to this theologian, is one's acquisition of the awareness that one can do nothing without the will of God. Thus, if man knows that he can only do something if God wills it, then he prays incessantly" (Mantzaridēs, *Deification of Man*, 91).

19. Ibid., 95

of prayer is "wordless, contemplative prayer," which is "the prayer in which the heart lays itself open in silence before God."[20] Lossky explains the process by which the believer transitions from spoken to "pure prayer":[21]

> Little by little the soul reintegrates itself, regains its unity, and particular petitions begin to disappear and seem superfluous, as God answers prayer by making manifest His all-embracing providence. There is an end of petition when the soul entrusts itself wholly to the will of God. This state is called 'pure prayer' (προσεθχή καθαρά). It is the end of πράζις, since nothing inconsistent with prayer can any longer gain access to the mind, nor turn aside the will which is now directed towards God, and united to the divine will.[22]

This pure form of prayer, which unites the believer with God's energies, first arises in the form of mystical ecstatic experiences, but eventually the worshipper becomes accustomed to the presence of God as a daily Christian reality.

The achievement of mystical experience is a synergistic process. Lossky claims: "As for vigils, prayers, alms, and other good works done in the name of Christ—these are the means whereby we acquire the Holy Spirit."[23] Although there is no strict notion of merit in the Eastern tradition,[24] Christian good works, which are primarily ascetic, do play a role in the acquisition of grace. Mantzaridēs is quick to qualify these types of statements, however, by arguing that "man's union with God and his deification are not the result of human activity but a gift of divine grace."[25] Prayer and asceticism do not merit grace, but they are channels through

20. Lossky, *Mystical Theology*, 206

21. "Pure prayer is a total cessation of thinking in the presence of divine mystery, before the descending of divine light in our mind" (Bartos, *Deification*, 29).

22. Lossky, *Mystical Theoloy*, 207.

23. Ibid., 196–97.

24. "The notion of merit is foreign to the Eastern tradition" (ibid., 197).

25. Mantzaridēs, *Deification of Man*, 88.

which Christians open themselves up to the reception of divine gifts. Lossky defines this Eastern approach to synergism by writing: "Grace is a presence of God within us which demands constant effort on our part; these efforts, however, in no way determine grace, nor does grace act upon our liberty as if it were external or foreign to it."[26] Augustine's influence was not predominant in the Eastern Church, and thus his theology of grace and the human will has not significantly affected Eastern Orthodox soteriology. Rather than the monergism of Augustinianism, the Eastern tradition has generally followed the thought of Saint John Cassian, who attempted to find a *via media* between strict Augustinianism and Pelagianism. Cassian argued that the human creature is fallen, and that divine grace is necessary, but the human will cooperates with grace in the process of redemption. This view was condemned in the West due to the influence of Saint Prosper of Aquitaine's moderate Augustinianism, which was defended at the Council of Orange in ad 529.

An Eastern approach to Christian living follows a standard of perfection that is to be sought by every believer. Isaac the Syrian argues that there are three stages of Christian life: patience, purification, and finally perfection. Lossky writes of this final stage, "It is a 'second regeneration' granted by the Father after baptism; a possibility of return to the Father; a continuous exodus from ourselves; a power which brings about the transformation of our nature."[27] This final stage of union is not, however, a completed goal. Christians do not achieve absolute spiritual perfection or sinlessness in this life. Repentance is a daily reality, and a necessary one for even the greatest saints. As Lossky notes, this view of perfection is connected to apophatic theology: "The more one is united to Him [God], the more one becomes aware of his unknowability, and, in the same way, the more perfect one becomes, the more one is aware of one's own imperfection."[28] In this manner, the Eastern Church is willing to confess with Luther that repentance

26. Lossky, *Mystical Theology*, 198.
27. Ibid., 204.
28. Ibid., 205.

is a daily reality for even the greatest saints, but remains much more optimistic about the level of spiritual perfection that can be achieved in this life than the Lutheran tradition would allow.

The Uncreated Light

At the center of the Hesychast debate between Barlaam and Palamas was the nature of visions of the "uncreated light." At Mount Athos, the Hesychasts sought to receive a vision of God, who is divine uncreated light. The image of light in reference to God is much more common in Eastern spirituality than in the West.[29] The presence of God is commonly said to be associated with light, especially in the act of the transfiguration on Mount Tabor (Matt 17:1–9; Mark 9:2–8, Luke 9:28–36). There are also Old Testament precedents for such an association, such as the light that shone on Moses' face after being in God's presence (Exod 34:29–35). This light is also seen by Paul on the Damascus road (Acts 9:3–9), and Stephen at the moment of his martyrdom (Acts 7:54–60).

Barlaam argued that such an experience of light was either a mere symbol of God, or an angelic presence. In contrast to this, Palamas purported that a vision of light is a display of the uncreated energies of God. Thus, for Barlaam, one could not see God, and thus light had to be a created essence, whereas for Palamas, believers could see God through his energies, and thus light is uncreated. Mantzaridēs states that "the hesychast monks of Mount Athos, in receiving the radiance of uncreated light, were experiencing direct communion with God, together with all the regenerative and deifying consequences of this."[30] These visions of God's energies have a deifying effect. Through God's energies, the soul is purified and communion with God is strengthened. In Palamas' view, this uncreated light is not perceptible by common human senses, for the faithful see the light only through spiritual transformation. The

---

29. This is partially due to the influence of Johannine theology in the East as opposed to the Pauline focus of Eastern theology. John commonly speaks of God in terms of light in opposition to darkness (1 John 1:5, John 8:12).

30. Mantzaridēs, *Deification of Man*, 99.

Holy Spirit grants believers the ability to see a spiritual reality that would otherwise be hidden from human view. At the transfiguration of Christ, the Apostles' spiritual senses were opened.[31] Thus, if an onlooker were to see the event through normal human perception, he or she would have seen nothing miraculous. Mantzaridēs writes:

> The vision of uncreated light by means of intellectual perception presents an analogy with the perception through the bodily eyes of created nature. In order to see the world around him, man requires, on the one hand, healthy eyesight, and on the other, the light of the sun. Only when the sun's brightness illuminates healthy eyes can man perceive the objects all about him. Similarly, perception of uncreated light requires both a purification of the intellectual vision and illumination from God.[32]

When people experience the uncreated light, it is primarily the intellect, rather than the body, that is transformed. Due to the influence of Dionysius, Palamas adopted the Platonic view of the intellect, which posits the νούς as the highest part of the human soul.[33] The intellect is capable of rising above itself, and must do so to achieve union with God. This occurs through mystical experience. The whole human—body included—is deified, but the deification of the body occurs through the instrumentality of the soul. The transformation that occurs through the uncreated light is eschatological in nature, for it prefigures the second coming of Christ and the resurrection of the body. In the eschatological state, this communion with the uncreated light continues, and Christians' progress in union with God extends throughout eternity due to the infinite nature of divinity.

31. "The reflection of the divine light can be seen by anyone, but not the divine light itself; for the latter you need the power of the Holy Spirit in your mind and body" (Bartos, *Deification*, 31).

32. Mantzaridēs, *Deification of Man*, 102.

33. "Reason is the faculty that rationalizes things and comprises definite concepts call reasons (*logoi*), while the mind is the faculty that thinks about contents. Thus the mind is the ultimate principle for everything in man, the basis of the human subject" (ibid., 29).

At work in this discussion is the distinction between divine essence and energies, which has been prominent in Palamite theology since the thirteenth century. Norman Russell expresses this approach to theology when he states:

> There are divine realities, or powers, in which created beings can participate. Such realities cannot therefore be the essence of God, yet are still in a real sense divine. These Gregory calls the energies. Their divinity is not derivative. That is to say, they do not exist "by participation." Nor are they distinct from God, like a fourth person of the Trinity, as his opponents claimed. The whole of God is present in each of his energies. And those who participate in them participate in the whole of God. Theosis is a gift of the Spirit, communicated through participation in the Spirit's deifying energy.[34]

This participation in divine energies protects the church against the idea that humanity can partake of the divine essence, and thus somehow become a person of the Holy Trinity.

Evaluation of the Apophatic Method

In studying Dionysius and the Palamite tradition, which drew on his neoplatonic ideology, it becomes apparent that there has been a major shift among theologians in terms of the orientation of theosis language. As was seen in the earlier fathers, deification was primarily viewed as an incarnational reality—part of the divine *oikonomia*. Through the incarnation, God united divinity with humanity in the person of Christ. Christ took upon himself, not the nature of a single individual, but humanity as a whole. Through Christ's incarnation, death, and resurrection, that which belongs properly to divinity is transferred to the human race. God took human frailty upon himself, and in turn, granted divine incorruptibility and immortality to humanity. In contrast to this economic approach, Dionysius places theosis in the realm of mystical experience, by which the Christian can commune with

---

34. Russell, *Fellow Workers with God*, 133.

God, who is beyond knowledge. Here we see a shift from theosis being first a redemptive historical reality and second an existential truth, to something that is almost exclusively mystical. Contemporary Eastern theologians have tended to blend these two means of discussing theosis, although though many theologians seem inclined to emphasize either the Christological or apophatic sense of deification.

The first question to be asked is whether apophaticism may be considered a valid theological method. The apophatic method has often been pitted against the "Western" approach to theology, by which is usually meant Thomism. The approach to God's being that Saint Thomas Aquinas takes, through the *analogia entis*, is opposed to the *via negativa* of the Areopogite.[35] Thomism views God on the basis of commonality between the creature and Creator. Through observing the goodness in created things, humanity is able to reason upward toward God, who embodies the perfection of these various attributes. Eastern theology, on the other hand, is based on the dissimilarity between creatures and their Creator, which argues that God is utterly transcendent beyond explanation or thought.

Lossky's formulation of these two differentiating approaches to theology fails to take into account the distinctive Reformational approaches to theology. Neither the Lutheran or Reformed theological traditions have adopted an *analogia entis* in the manner of Thomas. For the Lutheran theological tradition, especially in the writings of Luther himself, God is not to be known by way of negation or by an analogy of being, but by the revelation of his historical acts in Christ. Robert Jenson points out that "God's *identity* is told by his story with creatures"[36] and the manner in which God is to be known is through this story. The Bible begins not with a statement about God's essence—either by way of his transcendence or of his similarity with creation—but with a concrete action: "In the beginning God created the heavens and the earth" (Gen 1:1). God

---

35. See, for example, Lossky's discussion of this topic in *Mystical Theology*, 26–43.

36. Jenson, *Triune God*, 75, emphasis Jenson's.

is thus to be known as the one who *does*. He is known primarily as the one who redeems, that which Luther calls God's "proper work," but also as one who judges, which is God's "alien work."[37] In essence, God is the one who raised Jesus from the dead, in whom the forgiveness of sins is enacted.[38]

Now certainly, there are discussions of God's essence in the theology of the Reformation, for the Reformers adopted Orthodox Trinitarianism, which posits three persons and one divine essence.[39] However, there has been some reticence to proceed beyond the language of the ecumenical creeds on the doctrine of God. Francis Pieper, for example, even rejects the classic Augustinian discussion of the Trinity in terms of the Love, the Loved, and the act of Love itself as speculative.[40] This is not to say that Scholasticism nor even Thomism has had no influence on the Lutheran doctrine of God, since from the time of Gerhard there have been extensive discussions of the essence and attributes of God.[41] However, whatever valid place any discussion of God's essence and attributes may have, it must always be studied in view of God's acts in history. God is known primarily through his Trinitarian action, and knowledge of his essence and attributes is derived from his actions. Rather than arriving at an understanding of God either through means of negation or an analogy of being, Christians gain knowledge of God through the historical acts of Christ.

Luther's hidden and revealed God dialectic is essential to arriving at a Reformational approach to apophatic theology. Steven Paulson argues that when discussing the hidden God, Luther reveals himself as "an apophatic (negative) theologian of a different sort."[42] That which is negated, however, is not human language

---

37. Luther, *LW* 31:39–58.

38. For further discussion on this point, see Jenson, *Triune God*, 42–60.

39. *The Book of Concord* contains the so-called three Ecumenical Creeds: the Apostle's, Nicene, and Athanasian. The Augsburg Confession continues in this manner by including a summary of ancient Trinitarian dogma.

40. Pieper, *Christian Dogmatics*, 2:398–405.

41. See, for example, Gerhard, *Theological Commonplaces*.

42. Paulson, "Luther on the Hidden God," 364.

and expression, but the human *person*. Negation is "the act of God applying the cross to our very persons in this world."[43] Luther is not concerned with abstract philosophical speculation about the nature of God's essence. He is instead concerned with how God acts on the sinner in history. Paulson cites Luther as stating, "These theologians have wished to apprehend God through speculations and have paid no attention to the Word. I recommend that speculation be laid aside, and I should like to have this rule adhered to after my death."[44] Thus, Luther specifically rejected Dionysian apophaticism as speculative and unnecessary.

In some sense, Dionysius' assertion that God's essence is unknowable is a given in any philosophy of transcendent theism. Luther adopted the traditional Christian approach to divinity in the medieval period, which argued that God is a transcended being, simple, immutable, and impassible. Luther did not seek, as do many modern theologians, to reject classical theism for a God who is made more sensible or understandable to the human intellect. Luther utilizes the hidden and revealed God language in this context. God is in one sense unknowable, according to his transcended character and essence. However, God has revealed himself in the gospel. Richard Muller summarizes this doctrine by noting:

> the paradox of God's unknowability and self-manifestations as stated by Luther. The issue is not that God has been hidden and has now revealed himself, but rather that the revelation that has been given to man defies the wisdom of the world because it is the revelation of the hidden God. God is revealed in hiddenness and hidden in his revelation. He reveals himself paradoxically to thwart the proud, and *sub contrario*, under the opposite, omnipotence manifest on the cross.[45]

God's hiddenness is both the nature of his essence, and the manner by which he communicates himself. The God that human reason posits is utterly contrary to the manner in which God

43. Ibid.
44. Ibid., 365.
45. Muller, *Dictionary of Latin and Greek*, 90.

reveals himself. Rather than demonstrating his glory in a profound and visible manner, God comes to earth as a lowly human being who was put to death on a cross.

The Dyonisian tradition is not wrong in its emphasis on God's utter transcendence and the unknowability of the divine essence. The problem lies in what solution is posed to the hiddenness of God. Under the apophatic tradition, one's goal is to seek the hidden God in within oneself via prayer and negation of language and thought. In this manner, the soul seeks to find the hidden God as he is. For Luther, the solution is not to be found by delving deeper into the hidden God, but by looking to where God has revealed himself: in the gospel. This is the primary error that underlies Dionysius' method. The ancient fathers discussed here primarily looked not to the attributes of God in the abstract, but to the divine economy. They looked to the person and work of Christ to find where God meets his people.[46] This is what Luther—together with much of the following Reformation tradition—has done, and it seems clear from this discussion that Scripture supports this view.

The Validity of the Essence/Energies Distinction

Essential to the Palamite approach to the divine nature is the distinction between God's essence and energies, which has been discussed throughout the present work. The question of the validity of such a distinction must be asked in order to properly evaluate the neoplatonic form of deification as developed in the Eastern Church. According to the Neopalamite school, this distinction is necessary, because without this distinction, deification could be misconstrued to be the teaching that Christian believers become God in essence, rather than by participation. The assumption is that to participate in an essence is to become one with that essence. The Christian cannot participate in the divine essence, because to do so would mean that the Christian becomes divine by nature, which is contradictory to monotheism.

46. I do not mean to imply that the Eastern Church does not do this, simply that it does not have the central focus that it should.

As long as deification has been taught, theologians have been careful to distinguish a biblical from of deification from pagan concepts of apotheosis. However, early Christians did not feel the need to make a strict distinction between God's essence and energies. As was shown earlier, neither Irenaeus, nor Athanasius (the earliest writers who expounded upon this topic at length) made such a distinction in God, nor do most other patristic sources. It has been demonstrated that both Luther and Calvin spoke of theosis when commenting on 2 Pet 1:3–4, but that both were clear to distinguish partaking of the divine nature from becoming inherently divine. The Lutheran Orthodox followed this same pattern of thought. Joseph Stump, for example, states:

> The indwelling of God in the believer must not be understood in the pantheistic sense, as though the person of the believer were absorbed by Christ. On the contrary, it is a close personal union in which the believer rests in Christ and draws strength from Him . . . The mystery of this union finds its explanation in the faith which grasps Christ and makes Him its very own, and in the love which flows from that faith and binds the soul to Christ together in the most intimate and loving fellowship.[47]

All of these figures express the reality of participation in God without making the distinction between divine essence and energy. What the Palamite distinction amounts to is a speculative means of explaining how the believer participates in God without becoming God. The Lutheran dogmaticians were willing to admit both the truth of mystical union and the creature/Creator distinction without philosophizing about the manner in which these two truths coincide with one another. Ultimately, Palamite theology rests upon the unproven assumption that to participate in an essence is to become that essence. However, to participate in something necessarily distinguishes the one who participates from the one who is being participated in. Thus, the language of participation itself would imply a distinction between creature and Creator that is not to be confused. So it is that the Palamite

47. Stump, *Christian Faith*, 274.

distinction is one *possible* solution to the dilemma of participation without confusion, but is ultimately unnecessary.

The Experience of Mystical Union

Probably the most profound difference between the Eastern Orthodox and Lutheran traditions concerning theosis or mystical union concerns the application of this teaching in the Christian life. In this regard, the Eastern Orthodox Church encourages asceticism and contemplation, as well as the practice of Hesychastic prayer. This arises from the apophatic theology of the Eastern Church, whereby the way of negation is the manner in which Christians grow in knowledge of God and the experience of deification. This is also connected with the sought-after experience of the uncreated light, which arises from the distinction between God's essence and energies.

The Lutheran tradition is a liturgical one. Devotion through the liturgical life of the church is encouraged, as is the practice of the daily office and other forms of personal prayer. Some Lutherans (including the present author) have made use of the historic practice of utilizing prayer beads, for example. Unlike many in the broader Protestant world, Luther encouraged the use of written and memorized prayers, such as the morning and evening prayers included in his Small Catechism. Thus, the tradition of reciting the Jesus Prayer is consistent with Reformation spirituality. However, Luther was concerned with attaching God's actions to the means of grace: Word and Sacrament, rather than inward experience. It is through this strong connection between the presence of God and the means of grace that the Palamite tradition departs from the Lutheran.

Just as problematic, if not more so, for Luther than the Roman Catholic Church, was the Anabaptist movement. Luther condemned the Enthusiasts for promoting a view of salvation that is divorced from the means of grace. The Formula states: "Likewise we reject and condemn the error of the Enthusiasts, who contrive the idea that God draws people to himself, enlightens them, makes them righteous, and saves them without means, without the hearing of God's Word, even without the use of holy sacraments" (FC Ep II.13). The Eastern Church certainly does not divorce salvation from God's Word and Sacraments, but Luther saw traces of Enthusiasm even within sacramental traditions such as that of Roman Catholicism. He writes: "Therefore we should and must insist that God does not want to deal with us human beings, except by means of his external Word and sacrament" (SA VIII.10). This is the error of Islam and "even that of the Papists" (SA VIII.9). Although remaining strongly sacramental, the Dionysian tradition expounds upon a process of deification that is divorced from the means of grace, wherein the emphasis lies not on the external Word, but on the inner life of prayer.

The Christian should not seek for a direct experience of God, as in the vision of the uncreated light, because that is not God's manner of working. Rather, God works in his hiddenness, behind the means of Word and Sacrament. No experience of God is necessary aside from that of the liturgy, the preached Word, and the sacramental life of the church. It is through these means that the mystical union of the believer with God is strengthened and maintained. In a Lutheran mindset, there is no mystical experience to be sought after in personal prayer or contemplation; rather, union with God must be sought in the life of Christ, in which God united himself with humankind. Our consequent union with God arises only through Christ's incarnation and his presence in Word and Sacrament.

Conclusion

There are many similarities between the Eastern Orthodox doctrine of deification and the Lutheran teaching of mystical union. It has been demonstrated that every Christian theology has to wrestle with the question of theosis because of its prominence in the tradition of the church as well as its attestation in Scripture. This teaching has taken various forms throughout the centuries within different church traditions. For the Eastern Orthodox

Church, the Athanasian conviction that God became man so that man might become God was blended with a neoplatonic philosophy that culminated in the theology of Gregory Palamas. This was connected to experiential mysticism, and this form of deification became—and remains—the primary soteriological motif of the Eastern Church. The Lutheran tradition has followed the earlier fathers by emphasizing the divine economy, stressing the union between God and humankind as a Christological reality. This tradition was developed in the seventeenth-century Scholastic period under the name of "mystical union." This proposal that theosis is to be understood as "Christification" is an attempt to revitalize the teaching of mystical union within Lutheran Dogmatics in the hope that it might serve as a grounds for discussing its commonalities and differences with the Eastern Orthodox Church on the important topic of theosis. It is my hope that this work will promote productive theological dialogue between the two traditions in the coming years.

Bibliography

Ante-Nicene Fathers: The Writings of the Fathers down to AD 325. Edited by Alexandrer Roberts and James Donaldson. 10 vols. 1885–1887. Reprint, Peabody, MA: Hendrickson, 2004.

Arand, Charles P., et al. *The Lutheran Confessions: History and Theology of the Book of Concord*. Minneapolis: Fortress, 2012.

Athanasius, Saint, Patriarch of Alexandria. *On the Incarnation: The Treatise De Incarnatione Verbi Dei*. Edited and translated by Penelope Lawson. London: Mowbray, 1953.

Barker, Glen W., et al. *The New Testament Speaks*. San Francisco: Harper & Row, 1969.

Barnard, Leslie W. *Justin Martyr: His Life and Thought*. Cambridge: Cambridge University Press, 2008.

Bartos, Emil. *Deification in Eastern Orthodox Theology: An Evaluation and Critique of the Theology of Dumitru Stanilo*[set breve over second a]*ae*. Eugene, OR: Wipf & Stock, 1999.

Bauckham, Richard J. *Jude and 2 Peter*. Vol. 50 of *Word Biblical Commentary*. Waco, TX: Word, 1983.

Billings, J. Todd. "John Calvin: United to God Through Christ." In *Partakers of the Divine Nature: The History and Development of Deification in the Christian Traditions*, edited by Michael J. Christensen and Jeffrey A. Wittung, 200–218. Grand Rapids: Baker, 2007.

Braaten, Carl E., and Robert W. Jenson, eds. *Union with Christ: The New Finnish Interpretation of Luther*. Grand Rapids: Eerdmans, 1998.

Calvin, John. *Commentaries on the Catholic Epistles*. Edited and translated by and John Owen. Grand Rapids: Eerdmans, 1948.

Chemnitz, Martin. *The Two Natures in Christ*. Translated by J. A. O. Preus. Saint Louis: Concordia, 1971.

Chemnitz, Martin, and Johann Gerhard. *The Doctrine of Man in the Writings of Martin Chemnitz and Johann Gerhard*. Edited by Herman A. Preus and Edmund Smits, translated by Mario Colacci, et al. Saint Louis: Concordia, 2005.

Coniaris, Anthony M. *Achieving Your Potential in Christ, Theosis: Plain Talks on a Major Doctrine of Orthodoxy*. Rev. ed. Minneapolis: Light & Life, 2004.

———. *Introducing the Orthodox Church: Its Faith and Life*. Minneapolis: Light & Life, 1982.

Cooper, Jordan. "A Lutheran Response to Justification: Five Views." *Blogia Journal of Lutheran Theology* (2012) 1–6, http://logia.org/blogia/wp-content/uploads/2012/07/Cooper_Justification.pdf.

Bibliography

————. *The Righteousness of One: An Evaluation of Early Patristic Soteriology in Light of the New Perspective on Paul.* Eugene, OR: Wipf & Stock, 2013.

Dionysius, the Areopagite, Saint. *On the Divine Names and the Mystical Theology.* Translated by C. E. Rolt. Translations of Christian Literature Series 1 Greek Texts. New York: Macmillan, 1920.

Drewery, Ben. "Deification." In *Christian Spirituality: Essays in Honor of Gordon Rupp,* edited by Peter Brooks, 35–62. London: SCM, 1975.

Engelbrecht, Edward. *Friends of the Law: Luther's Use of the Law for the Christian Life.* Saint Louis: Concordia, 2011.

Finch, Jeffrey D. "Neo-Palamism, Divinizing Grace, and the Breach between East and West." In *Partakers of the Divine Nature: The History and Development of Deification in the Christian Traditions,* edited by Michael J. Christensen and Jeffrey A. Wittung, 233–49. Grand Rapids: Baker, 2007.

————. "Irenaeus on the Christological Basis of Human Divinization." In *Deification in Christian Theology,* edited by Vladimir Kharlamov, 86–103. Vol. 2 of *Theosis.* Princeton Theological Monograph Series 156. Eugene, OR: Pickwick, 2011.

Finlan, Stephen. "Can We Speak of *Theosis* in Paul?" In *Partakers of the Divine Nature: The History and Development of Deification in the Christian Traditions,* edited by Michael J. Christensen and Jeffrey A. Wittung, 68–80. Grand Rapids: Baker, 2007.

————. "Deification in Jesus' Teaching." In *Deification in Christian Theology,* edited by Vladimir Kharlamov, 21–41. Vol. 2 of *Theosis.* Princeton Theological Monograph Series 156. Eugene, OR: Pickwick, 2011.

————. "Second Peter's Notion of Divine Participation." In *The[set macron over o]osis: Deification in Christian Theology,* edited by Stephen Finlan Vladimir Kharlamov, 32–50. Princeton Theological Monograph Series 52. Eugene, OR: Pickwick, 2006.

Franzmann, Martin H. *The Word of the Lord Grows: An Introduction to the Origin, Purpose, and Meaning of the New Testament.* Saint Louis: Concordia, 1961.

Gathercole, Simon J. *Where Is Boasting? Early Jewish Soteriology and Paul's Response in Romans 1–5.* Grand Rapids: Eerdmans, 2002.

Gerberding, George Henry. *The Way of Salvation in the Lutheran Church.* Philadelphia: General Council, 1917.

Gerhard, Johan. *Theological Commonplaces: On the Nature of God and on the Most Holy Mystery of the Trinity.* Edited by Benjamin T. G. Mayes and translated by Richard J. Dinda. Saint Louis: Concordia, 2007.

Gorman, Michael J. *Inhabiting the Cruciform God: Kenosis, Justification, and Theosis in Paul's Narrative Soteriology.* Grand Rapids: Eerdmans, 2009.

Hodge, Charles. *Systematic Theology.* 3 vols. Peabody: Hendrickson, 2003.

Hoenecke, Adolf. *Evangelical Lutheran Dogmatics.* 4 vols. Milwaukee: Northwestern, 1999–2009.

Holms, Michael W., ed and trans. *Apostolic Fathers: Greek Texts and English Translations.* Grand Rapids: Baker, 1992.

Jenson, Robert W. *The Triune God*. Vol. 1 of *Systematic Theology*. New York: Oxford, 1997.

Kärkkäinen, Veli-Matti. *One with God: Salvation as Deification and Justification*. Unitas Books. Collegeville, MN: Liturgical, 2004.

Keating, Daniel A. *Deification and Grace*. Introductions to Catholic Doctrine. Naples, FL: Sapientia, 2007.

Kharlamov, Vladimir. "Emergence of the Deification Theme in the Apostolic Fathers." In vol. 1 of *The*[set macron over o]*osis: Deification in Christian Theology*, edited by Stephen Finlan and Vladimir Kharlamov, 51–66. Princeton Theological Monograph Series 52. Eugene, OR: Pickwick, 2006.

————. "Deification in the Apologists of the Second Century." In vol. 1 of *The*[set macron over o]*osis: Deification in Christian Theology*, edited by Stephen Finlan and Vladimir Kharlamov, 67–85. Princeton Theological Monograph Series 52. Eugene, OR: Pickwick, 2006.

Kilcrease, Jack D. *Self-Donation of God: A Contemporary Lutheran Approach to Christ and His Benefits*. Eugene, OR: Wipf & Stock, 2013.

Kolb, Robert, and Timothy J. Wengert, eds. *The Book of Concord: The Confessions of the Evangelical Lutheran Church*. Translated by Charles Arand, et al. Minneapolis: Fortress, 2000.

Krill, Philip. *Life in the Trinity: A Catholic Vision of Communion and Deification*. Raleigh, NC: Lulu, 2010.

Kruger, Michael J. "The Authenticity of 2 Peter." *Journal of the Evangelical Theological Society* 42 (1999) 645–71.

Lenz, John R. "Deification of the Philosopher in Classical Greece." In *Partakers of the Divine Nature: The History and Development of Deification in the Christian Traditions*, edited by Michael J. Christensen and Jeffrey A. Wittung, 47–67. Grand Rapids: Baker, 2007.

Lossky, Vladimir. *In the Image and Likeness of God*. Edited by John H. Erickson and Thomas E. Bird. Crestwood, NY: Saint Vladimir's Seminary Press, 1974.

————. *The Mystical Theology of the Eastern Church*. Crestwood, NY: Saint Vladimir's Seminary Press, 1976.

————. *Orthodox Theology: An Introduction*. Translated by Ian and Ihita Kesarcodi-Watson. Crestwood, NY: Saint Vladimir's Seminary Press, 1978.

Louth, Andrew. "The Place of Theosis in Orthodox Theology." In *Partakers of the Divine Nature: The History and Development of Deification in the Christian Traditions*, edited by Michael J. Christensen and Jeffrey A. Wittung, 32–45. Grand Rapids: Baker, 2007.

Luther, Martin. *Commentary on Peter and Jude*. Edited and translated by John Nichols Lenker. Luther Classic Commentaries. Grand Rapids: Kregel, 2005.

————.*Career of the Reformer 1*. Edited by Harold J. Grimm and Helmut T. Lehmann. Vol. 31 of *Luther's Works*. Philadelphia: Fortress, 1957.

Bibliography

———. *D. Martin Luthers Werk; Kritische Gesamtausgabe.* Weimarer Ausgabe [Weimar Edition]. 65 vols. Weimar, Germany: Böhlau, 1883–1993.

———. *Lectures on Galatians: Chapters 1–4.* Edited by Jaroslav Pelikan. Vol. 26 of *Luther's Works.* Saint Louis: Concordia, 1963.

———. *Lectures on Galatians: Chapters 5–6.* Edited by Jaroslav Pelikan. Vol. 27 of *Luther's Works.* Saint Louis: Concordia, 1964.

Mannermaa, Tuomo. *Christ Present in Faith: Luther's View of Justification.* Edited and translated by Kirsi Irmeli Stjerna. Minneapolis: Fortress, 2005.

———. *Two Kinds of Love: Martin Luther's Religious World.* Edited and translated by Kirsi Irmeli Stjerna. Minneapolis: Fortress, 2010.

Mantzarid[set macron over e]es, Ge[set macron over first o]orgios I. *The Deification of Man: Saint Gregory Palamas and the Orthodox Tradition.* Contemporary Greek Theologians 2. Crestwood, NY: Saint Vladimir's Seminary Press, 1984.

Marquart, Kurt E. "Luther and Theosis." *Concordia Theological Quarterly* 64 (2000) 182–205.

Mattox, Mickey Leland, and A. G. Roeber. *Changing Churches: An Orthodox, Catholic, and Lutheran Theological Conversation.* Grand Rapids: Eerdmans, 2012.

Meyendorff, John, and Robert Tobias, eds. *Salvation in Christ: A Lutheran-Orthodox Dialogue.* Minneapolis: Augsburg, 1992.

Mosser, Carl. "The Greatest Possible Blessing: Calvin and Deification." *Scottish Journal of Theology* 55 (2002) 36–57.

Muller, Richard A. *Dictionary of Latin and Greek Theological Terms: Drawn Principally from Protestant Scholastic Theology.* Grand Rapids: Baker, 2006.

Nellas, Panayiotis. *Deification in Christ: Orthodox Perspectives on the Nature of the Human Person.* Translated by Norman Russell. Contemporary Greek Theologians 5. Crestwood, NY: Saint Vladimir's Seminary Press, 1987.

Nicene and Post-Nicene Fathers, Series 1. Edited by Philip Schaff. 14 vols. 1886–1889. Reprint, Peabody, MA: Hendrickson, 2004.

———, Series 2. Edited by Philip Schaff and Henry Wace. 14 vols. 1890–1900. Reprint, Peabody, MA: Hendrickson, 2004.

Palamas, Saint Gregory. *The Triads.* Edited by John Meyendorff and translated by Nicholas Gendle. Classics of Western Spirituality. New York: Paulist, 1983.

Parvis, Sarah, and Paul Foster, eds. *Justin Martyr and His Worlds.* Minneapolis: Fortress, 2007.

Paulson, Steven D. "Luther on the Hidden God." *Word and World* 19 (1999) 363–71.

Perl, Eric David. *Theophany: The Neoplatonic Philosophy of Dionysius the Areopagite.* SUNY Series in Ancient Greek Philosophy. Albany: State University of New York Press, 2007.

Pieper, Francis. *Christian Dogmatics.* 4 vols. Saint Louis: Concordia, 1950–1957.

Popov, Ivan V. "The Idea of Deification in the Early Eastern Church." In *Deification in Christian Theology,* edited by Vladimir Kharlamov, 42–82.

Vol. 2 of *Theosis*. Princeton Theological Monograph Series 156. Eugene, OR: Pickwick, 2011

Prues, Robert D., and Wilbert H. Rosin. *A Contemporary Look at the Formula of Concord*. Saint Louis: Concordia, 1978.

Quasten, Johannes. *Patrology*. 4 vols. Notre Dame: Christian Classics, 1986.

Russell, Norman. *Fellow Workers with God: Orthodox Thinking on Theosis*. Foundations Series 5. Crestwood: Saint Vladimir's Seminary Press, 2009.

Sanders, E. P. *Paul and Palestinian Judaism: A Comparison of Patterns of Religion*. Philadelphia: Fortress, 1977.

Schmid, Heinrich. *The Doctrinal Theology of the Evangelical Lutheran Church, Exhibited and Verified from the Original Sources*. Translated by Henry Eyster Jacobs and Charles A. Hay. Philadelphia: Lutheran Publication Society, 1876.

Schreiner, Thomas R. "Justification: The Saving Righteousness of God in Christ." *Journal of the Evangelical Theological Society* 54 (2011) 19–34.

———. *The Law and Its Fulfillment: A Pauline Theology of Law*. Grand Rapids: Baker, 1998.

Schumacher, William W. *"Who Do I Say That You Are?" Anthropology and the Theology of Theosis in the Finnish School of Tuomo Mannermaa*. Eugene, OR: Wipf & Stock, 2010.

Schweitzer, Albert. *The Mysticism of Paul the Apostle*. Translated by William Montgomery. Baltimore: John Hopkins, 1998.

———. *The Quest of the Historical Jesus: A Critical Study of its Progress from Reimarus to Wrede*. Albert Schweitzer Library. Baltimore: John Hopkins, 1998.

St[set breve over first a]aniloae, Dumitru. *Revelation and Knowledge of the Triune God*. Vol. 1 of *The Experience of God: Orthodox Dogmatic Theology*. Translated and edited by Ioan Ionit[set breve over a]a and Robert Barringer. Brookline, MA: Holy Cross Orthodox, 1998.

———. *The World: Creation and Deification*. Vol. 2 of *The Experience of God: Orthodox Dogmatic Theology*. Translated and edited by Ioan Ionit[set breve over a]a and Robert Barringer. Brookline, MA: Holy Cross Orthodox, 2000.

Starr, James. "Does 2 Peter 1:4 Speak of Deification?" In *Partakers of the Divine Nature: The History and Development of Deification in the Christian Traditions*, edited by Michael J. Christensen and Jeffrey A. Wittung, 81–94. Grand Rapids: Baker, 2007.

Stucco, Guido. *Not without Us: A Brief History of the Forgotten Catholic Doctrine of Predestination during the Semipelagian Controversy*. Tucson, AZ: Fenestra, 2006.

Stump, Joseph. *The Christian Faith: A System of Christian Dogmatics*. Philadelphia: Muhlenberg, 1942.

Vainio, Olli-Pekka. *Engaging Luther: A (New) Theological Assessment*. Eugene, OR: Cascade, 2010.

Bibliography

————. *Justification and Participation in Christ: The Development of the Lutheran Doctrine of Justification from Luther to the Formula of Concord* (1580). Studies in Medieval and Reformation Traditions 130. Boston: Brill, 2008.

Vickers, Brian. *Jesus' Blood and Righteousness: Paul's Theology of Imputation.* Wheaton, IL: Crossway, 2006.

Voigt, Andrew George. *Biblical Dogmatics.* Columbia, SC: Lutheran Board of Publication, 1917.

Von Harnack, Adolf. *History of Dogma.* 7 vols. Translated by Neil Buchanan. New York: Dover, 1961.

Walther, C. F. W. *The Proper Distinction between Law and Gospel.* Translated by W. H. T. Dau. Saint Louis: Concordia, 1986.

Ware, Kallistos, Bishop of Diokleia. *The Orthodox Church.* Penguin Religion and Mythology. London: Penguin, 1997.

Wedgeworth, Steven. "Reforming Deification." *Credenda Agenda.* January 5, 2011. http://www.credenda.org/index.php/Theology/reforming-deification.html.

Westerholm, Stephen. *Perspectives Old and New on Paul: The "Lutheran" Paul and His Critics.* Grand Rapids: Eerdmans, 2004.

Wilson, Daniel E. *Deification and the Rule of Faith: The Communication of the Gospel in Hellenistic Culture.* Bloomington, IN: CrossBooks, 2010.

Wingren, Gustaf. *Man and the Incarnation: A Study in the Biblical Theology of Irenaeus.* Translated by Ross Mackenzie. Eugene, OR: Wipf & Stock, 2004.

Made in the USA
Middletown, DE
22 April 2022

64632969R00080